D0342013

Introduction

This pocket edition of the Bhagavad Gītā is specially meant for those who do not know the Devanāgarī script and would like to have the Text in Roman script with a plain English translation. It will be useful also for those who want to carry a great scripture even to their work spot in order to seek holy company in the midst of work.

Though put in the context of a battle scene, the object of the Gītā is not war - mongering but exhorting man to do his duty, whatever it be, in a spirit of detachment and dedication. Such an attitude can be sustained only if a man has unreserved faith in God and in His supremacy over the destiny of man individually and of the cosmos as a whole. So beginning with an exhortation to action, the Gītā gives in substantiation of that teaching a universal theology without any sectarian or dogmatic stance, which would be found congenial by all who are not in the grip of those narrow loyalties. For this reason we have designated it as the scripture of mankind.

Speaking about the universality and profundity of the teachings of the

Gītā, Warren Hastings, the first Governor-General of India (1773-1784), in his Introduction to the first-ever English translation of the Text by Charles Wilkins (1784) declares that 'Works as the Gītā could live long after the British domination in India has ceased to exist' and that it contains passages 'elevated to a track of sublimity into which our habits of judgement will find it difficult to penetrate'.

A study of this small Text of seven hundred verses will convince any one that such an encomium of the wisdom contained in it is not a misplaced over-estimate.

KEY TO PRONUNCIATION

Sounds like	
a	o in son
ā	a in master
i	i in if
ī	ee in feel
u	u in full
ū	oo in boot
ṛ	somewhat between r an ri
e	ay in May
ai	y in my

KEY TO PRONUNCIATION

o	o in oh
au	ow in now
k	k in keen
kh	ckh in blockhead
g	g (hard) in go
gh	gh in log-hut
ṅ	ng in singer
c	ch (not k) chain
ch	chh in catch him
j	j in judge
jh	dgeh in hedgehog
ñ	n (somewhat) as in French
ṭ	t tn ten

th	th in ant-hill
ḍ	d in den
ḍh	dh in godhood
ṇ	n in under
t	t in French
th	th in thumb
d	th in then
dh	then in breathe
n	n in not
p	p in pen
ph	ph in loop-hole
b	b in bag
bh	bh in abhor
m	m in mother

y	y in yard
r	r in run
l	l in luck
v	v in avert
ś	sh in reich (German)
ṣ	sh in show
s	s in sun
h	in hot
ṁ	m in sum
ḥ	h in half

Chapter I

Arjuna's Conversion

Dhṛtarāṣṭra Uvāca:
Dharma-kṣetre kuru-kṣetre
samavetā yuyutsavaḥ /
māmakāḥ pāṇḍavāścaiva
kim akurvata, Sañjaya // 1

Dhṛtarāṣṭra said:

O Sañjaya! What indeed did my people and the followers of the Pāṇḍavas do after having assembled in the holy land of Kurukṣetra, eager to join battle?

Sañjaya uvāca:
Dṛṣṭvā tu pāṇḍavānīkaṁ
vyūḍhaṁ duryodhanas tadā /
ācāryam upasaṅgamya
rājā vacanam abravīt // 2

Sañjaya said:

Then seeing the army of the Pāṇdavas arrayed in battle order, King Duryodhana for his part approached the teacher Droṇa and spoke to him the following words:

Paśyaitāṁ pāṇḍu-putrāṇām
ācārya mahatīṁ camūm /
vyūḍhāṁ drupada-putreṇa
tava śiṣeṇa dhīmatā // 3

O Teacher! Behold this great army of the sons of Pāṇdu, arrayed in battle order by your talented disciple, the son of Drupada.

Atra śūrā maheṣvāsā
Bhīmārjuna-samā yudhi /
Yuyudhāno Virāṭaśca
Drupadaś ca mahā-rathaḥ // 4

Here (in that army) are many brave bow-men of note who are equal to Bhima and Arjuna in battle — great car-warriors like Yuyudhāna, Virāṭa and Drupada;

Dhṛṣṭaketuś Cekitānaḥ
Kāśi-rājaś ca vīryavān /

Purujit Kuntibhojaś ca
Śaibyaś ca nara-puṅgavaḥ // 5

Dhṛṣṭaketu, Cekitāna and the brave king of Kāśi; Purujit, Kuntibhoja and Śaibya the best of men;

Yudhāmanyuś ca vikrānta
Uttamaujāś ca vīryavān /
Saubhadro Draupadeyāś ca
sarva eva mahā-rathāḥ // 6

The powerful Yudhāmanyu, the brave Uttamauja, the son of Subhadra, and the sons of Draupadi — all these are indeed noted car-warriors.

Asmākaṁ tu viśiṣṭā ye
tān nibodha dvij' ottama /
nāyakā mama sainyasya
saṁjñ' ārthaṁ tān bravīmi te // 7

O best of Brāhmaṇas, I shall mention for your information the names of the distinguished leaders of our army.

Bhavān Bhīṣmaś ca Karṇaś ca
Kṛpaś ca samitiñ-jayaḥ /
Aśvatthāmā Vikarṇaś ca
Saumadattir Jayadrathaḥ // 8

Yourself, Bhīṣma and Karṇa, the victorious Kṛpa, Aswatthāmā,

Vikarṇa and Jayadratha the son of Somadatta.

Anye ca bahavaḥ śūrā
mad-arthe tyakta-Jīvitāḥ /
nānā-śastra praharaṇāḥ
sarve yuddha-viśaradāḥ // 9

These and many more brave men, who are ready to lay down their lives for my sake and who fight with various types of weapons, are present here. All of them are seasoned warriors.

Aparyāptaṁ tad asmākaṁ
balaṁ Bhīṣm' ābhirakṣitam /
paryāptaṁ tv idam eteṣāṁ
balaṁ Bhīm' ābhirakṣitam // 10

Though numerically superior, inadequate is the army of ours defended by Bhīṣma, while theirs guarded by Bhīma is adequate.

Ayaneṣu ca sarveṣu
yathā-bhāgam avasthitāḥ /
Bhīṣmam evābhirakṣantu
bhavantaḥ sarva eva hi // 11

Therefore do ye all protect Bhīṣma remaining in appropriate positions in your respective divisions.

Tasya sañjanayan harṣaṁ
Kuru-vṛddhaḥ pitāmahaḥ /
siṁha-nādaṁ vinady' occaiḥ
śaṅkhaṁ dadhmau pratāpavān // 12

Cheering him up, the valiant grandfather Bhīṣma, the oldest of the Kurus, sounded a lion-roar loudly and blew his conch-shell horn.

Tataḥ śaṅkhāś ca bheryaś ca
paṇav' ānaka-gomukhāḥ /
sahas'aiv'ābhyahanyanta
sa śabdas tumulo'bhavat // 13

Thereupon, conchs, kettle-drums, tabors, trumpets, and cowhorns all blared out suddenly causing a tremendous sound.

Tataḥ śvetair hayair yukte
mahati syandane sthitau /

Mādhavaḥ Pāṇḍavaś c'aiva
divyau śaṅkhau pradadhmatuḥ // 14

Then Sri Kṛṣṇa and Arjuna, seated in a great chariot with white horses yoked to it, blew their celestial conch-shell horns.

Pāñcajanyaṁ Hṛṣīkeśo
Devadattaṁ Dhanañjayaḥ /
Pauṇḍraṁ dadhmau mahā-śaṅkham
bhīma-karmā Vṛk'odaraḥ // 15

Sri Kṛṣṇa blew his conch Pāñcajanya, Arjuna blew Devadatta, and Bhīma of terrible deeds sounded his great conch Pauṇḍra.

Anantavijayaṁ rājā
Kuntī-putro Yudhiṣṭhiraḥ /
Nakulaḥ Sahadevaś ca
Sughoṣa-Maṇipuṣpakau // 16

Raja Yudhiṣṭhira, the son of Kuntī, blew his conch Anantavijaya, and Nakula and Sahadeva, Sughoṣa and Maṇipuṣpaka respectively.

Kāśyaś ca param'eṣvāsaḥ
Śikhaṇḍī ca mahā-rathaḥ /
Dhṛṣṭadyumno Virāṭaś ca
Sātyakiś c'āparājitaḥ // 17

The great archer, king of Kāśi, the mighty car-warrior Śikhaṇḍī and Dhṛṣṭadyumna and invincible Sātyaki;

Drupado Draupadeyāś ca
sarvaśaḥ pṛthivī-pate /
Saubhadraś ca mahā-bāhuḥ
śaṅkhān dadhmuḥ pṛthak
pṛthak // 18

The King of Drupada, the sons of Draupadī, the mighty armed son of Subhadrā — all these, O king, sounded their conchshell horns again and again everywhere.

Sa ghoṣo Dhārtarāṣṭrāṇāṁ
hṛdayāni vyadārayat /
nabhaś ca pṛthivīṁ c'aiva
tumulo vyanunādayan // 19

That tumultuous uproar, resounding in the sky and over the land, pierced the hearts of the followers of Dhṛtarāṣṭra.

Atha vyavasthitān dṛṣṭvā
Dhārtarāṣṭrān kapi-dhvajaḥ /
pravṛtte śastra-sampāte
dhanur udyamya Pāṇḍavaḥ /
Hṛṣīkeśaṁ tadā vākyam
idam āha mahīpate // 20-21

O King! Arjuna, the Pāṇḍava-leader with the banner crest of a monkey, on seeing the followers of Dhṛtarāṣṭra arrayed for battle and the clash of weapons about to start, held up his bow and said the following words to Śrī Kṛṣṇa:

Arjuna uvāca:

Senayor ubhayor madhye
rathaṁ sthāpaya me'cyuta /
yāvad etān nirīkṣe'haṁ
yoddhu-kāmān avasthitān /
kair mayā saha yoddhavyam
asmin raṇa-samudyame // 21-22

Arjuna said:

O Acyuta! Please station my chariot between the two armies so that I may have a view, on the eve of this battle, of all those standing ready to fight, and learn who all are the persons with whom I have to contend.

Yotsyamānān avekṣe'ham
ya ete'tra samāgatāḥ /
Dhārtarāṣṭrasya durbuddher
yuddhe priyacikīrṣavaḥ // 23

Let me see all those who have arrived to favour the evil-minded son of Dhṛtarṣāṭra in war and are standing ready to join battle.

Sañjaya uvāca:

Evam ukto Hṛṣīkeśo
Guḍākeśena Bhārata /
senayor ubhayor madhye
sthāpayitvā rath'ottamam //

Bhīṣma-Droṇa pramukhataḥ
sarveṣāṁ ca mahī-kṣitām
uvāca Pārtha paśy'aitān
samavetān Kurūn iti //24-25

Sañjaya said:

O King Dhṛtarāṣṭra! Śrī Kṛṣṇa, to whom Arjuna addressed these words, stationed that most splendid of chariots at a place between the two armies, confronting Bhīṣma, Droṇa and all those chiefs, and said: "O Arjuna! See these men of the Kuru horde assembled for battle."

Tatr'āpaśyat sthitān Pārthaḥ
pitṛn atha pitāmahān /

ācāryān mātulān bhrātṛn
putrān pautrān sakhīṁs tathā //

Śvaśurān suhṛdaś caiva
senayor ubhayor api /
tān samīkṣya sa Kaunteyaḥ
sarvān bandhūn avasthitān //
kṛpayā paray'āviṣṭo
viṣīdann idam abravīt / 26-27

There he saw standing in both the armies — fathers, grand-fathers, uncles, brothers, sons, grandsons, comrades, fathers-in-law and bosom friends. Seeing all these kinsmen arrayed, Arjuna was overcome with great pity, and said sorrowing:

Arjuna uvāca:

Dṛṣṭvemaṁ svajanaṁ Kṛṣṇa
yuyutsuṁ samupasthitam //
Sīdanti mama gātrāṇi
mukhaṁ ca pariśuṣyati /
vepathuś ca śarīre me
roma-harṣaś ca jāyate // 28-29

Arjuna said:

Seeing these relatives standing eager to join battle, my limbs are giving way, my mouth is parching. I get trembling of the body and horripilations.

Gāṇḍīvaṁ sraṁsate hastāt
tvakc'aiva paridahyate

na ca śaknomy avasthātuṁ
bhramatī'va ca me manaḥ // 30

My bow Gāṇḍīva is slipping from my hand. My skin too is burning. I find it impossible to stand firm, and my mind is, as it were, reeling.

Nimittāni ca paśyāmi
viparītāni Keśava /
na ca śreyo'nupaśyāmi
hatvā svajanam āhave // 31

O Keśava! I see adverse omens. I do not feel that any good will come by killing all one's kinsmen in battle.

Na kāṅkṣe vijayaṁ Kṛṣṇa
na ca rājyaṁ sukhāni ca /

kim no rājyena Govinda
kiṁ bhogair jīvitena vā // 32

O Kṛṣṇa! I do not long for victory, or kingdom, or enjoyments. O Govinda! Of what use is kingdom, enjoyments or even life itself?

Yeṣām arthe kāṅkṣitaṁ no
rājyaṁ bhogāḥ sukhāni ca /
ta ime'vasthitā yuddhe
prāṇāṁs tyaktvā dhanāni ca //
Ācāryāḥ pitaraḥ putrāḥ
tathaiva ca pitāmahāḥ /
mātulāḥ śvaśsurāḥ pautrāḥ
śyālāḥ saṁbandhinas tathā // 33-34

Those for whose sake kingdoms, enjoyments, and pleasures are desired — those very teachers, fathers and sons, as also grandfathers, uncles, fathers-in-law and other relatives are here stationed in battle ready to give up their lives and possessions.

Etān na hantum icchāmi
ghnato'pi Madhusūdana /
api trailokya-rājyasya
hetoḥ kiṁ nu mahīkṛte // 35

Even for the sovereignty of the three worlds, I do not desire to kill them, though myself killed — how much less then for this earthly kingdom!

Nihatya Dhārtarāṣṭrān naḥ
kā prītiḥ syāj Janārdana /
pāpam ev'āśrayed asmān
hatv' aitān ātatāyinaḥ // 36

What joy can there be for us by killing these sons of Dhṛtarāṣṭra? Though they are murderous villains, only sin will accrue to us by killing them.

Tasmān n'ārhā vayaṁ hantuṁ
Dhārtarāṣṭrān svabāndhavān /
svajanaṁ hi kathaṁ hatvā
sukhinaḥ syāma Mādhava // 37

Therefore, O Mādhava! it is not befitting that we kill our relations, the sons of Dhṛtarāṣṭra. How could one be happy by the slaughter of one's own kinsmen?

Yady apy ete na paśyanti
lobh'opahata-cetasḥ /
kula-kṣaya-kṛtaṁ doṣaṁ
mitra-drohe ca pātakam //

Kathaṁ na jñeyam asmābhiḥ
pāpād asmān nivartitum
kula-kṣaya-kṛtaṁ doṣam
prapaśyadbhir Janārdana // 38-39

O Janārdana! Even if these people, with their intelligence overpowered by greed, do not see any evil in the decay of families and any sin in the persecution of friends, why should not we, who are aware of the evil of such decay of families, learn to desist from that sin?

Kula-kṣaye praṇaśyanti
kula-dharmāḥ sanātanāḥ
dharme naṣṭe kulaṁ kṛtsnam
adharmo' bhibhavatyuta // 40

When a clan becomes decadent, its ancient traditions (laws) perish. When traditions perish, the entire clan is indeed overcome by lawlessness.

Adharm'ābhibhavāt Kṛṣṇa
praduṣyanti kula-striyaḥ /

strīṣu duṣṭāsu Vārṣṇeya
jāyate varṇa-saṅkaraḥ // 41

O Kṛṣṇa! When lawlessness prevails, the women of the clans become corrupt. O scion of the Vṛṣṇis! When women are corrupted, mixture of classes (promiscuity) prevails.

Saṅkaro narakāy' aiva
kula-ghnānāṁ kulasya ca
patanti pitaro hy eṣāṁ
lupta-piṇḍ'odaka-kriyāḥ // 42

Promiscuity results only in hell to those destroyers of the clans, as also to the members of the clan. For (being without legitimate progeny to perform obsequies), the spirits of their ancestors fall, deprived of the offerings of rice ball and water.

Doṣair etaiḥ kula-ghnānāṁ
varṇa-saṅkara-kārakaiḥ /
utsādyante jāti-dharmāḥ
kula-dharmāś ca śāśvatāḥ // 43

By the misdeeds of these ruiners of clans and promoters of promiscuity, the immemorial traditions of the communities and clans are uprooted.

Utsanna-kula-dharmāṇāṁ
manuṣyāṇāṁ Janārdana /
narake niyataṁ vāso
bhavatī'ty anuśuśruma // 44

O Janārdana! We have heard that residence in hell awaits men, the religious traditions of whose clans have been destroyed.

Aho bata mahat pāpaṁ
kartuṁ vyavasitā vayam /
yad rājya-sukha-lobhena
hantuṁ svajanam udyatāḥ // 45

Alas! What great sin have we resolved to commit when we prepared ourselves to destroy our kinsmen out of greed for the pleasures of a kingdom!

Yadi mām apratīkāram
aśastraṁ śastra-pāṇayaḥ /

Dhārtarāṣṭrā raṇe hanyuḥ
tan me kṣemataraṁ bhavet // 46

Far better would it be for me if the sons of Dhṛtarāṣṭra, with weapons in hand, kill me in battle, unarmed and unresisting!

Sañjaya uvāca:
Evam uktvārjunaḥ saṁkhye
rathopastha upāviśat /
visṛjya saśaraṁ cāpaṁ
śoka-saṁvigna-mānasaḥ // 47

Sañjaya said:

So saying, Arjuna, with his mind overwhelmed with sorrow, abandoned his bow and arrows and sat down on the chariot seat.

Chapter II

Yoga of Knowledge

Sañjaya uvāca:

Taṁ tathā kṛpayā'viṣṭam
aśru-pūrṇākul'ekṣaṇam /
viṣīdantaṁ idam vākyam
uvāca Madhusūdanaḥ // 1

Sañjaya said:

To him who was thus overcome with pity and whose eyes were full of tears and bore a bewildered look, Sri Kṛṣṇa spoke as follows:

Śrī Bhagavān uvāca:

Kutas tvā kaśmalam idaṁ
viṣame samupasthitam /
anārya-juṣṭam asvargyam
akīrtikaram Arjuna // 2

The Blessed Lord said:

O Arjuna! Whence has this loathsome stupidity come upon you in this crisis? It (this attitude) is unworthy of a noble personage; it is a bar to heaven and a cause of much disrepute.

Klaibyaṁ māsma gamaḥ Pārtha
naitat tvayy upapadyate!
kṣudraṁ hṛdaya-daurbalyaṁ
tyaktv' ottiṣṭha paraṁtapa // 3

O Pārtha! Yield not to unmanliness! It befits thee not. Abandoning this base faint-heartedness, rise up, O dreaded hero!

Arjuna uvāca:

Kathaṁ Bhīṣmaṁ ahaṁ saṁkhye
Droṇaṁ ca Madhusūdana /
iṣubhiḥ pratiyotsyāmi
puj' ārhāv arisūdana // 4

Arjuna said:

O Kṛṣṇa! How can I attack Bhīṣma and Droṇa in battle with my arrows? They are, indeed worthy of worship, O destroyer of foes!

Gurūn ahatvā-hi mahā' nubhāvān
śreyo bhoktuṁ bhaikṣyam apī ha loke /
hatvā'rtha kāmāṁs tu gurūn ih' aiva
bhuñjīya bhogān
rudhirapradigdhān // 5

It is indeed better to live here in this world on a beggar's fare than to prosper by killing these venerable teachers. The enjoyment of pleasure and power obtained through the slaughter of these teachers and elders will surely be bloodstained.

Na c'aitad vidmaḥ kataran no garīyo
yad vā jayema yadi vāno jayeyuḥ /

yān eva hatvā na jijīviṣāmas
te' vasthitāḥ pramukhe
Dhārtarāṣṭrāḥ // 6

We do not know which of the two (alternatives) will be the better — the one that we should conquer them or the other that they should conquer us. The men on the side of Dhritrāṣṭra, standing arrayed against us, are the very people after killing whom we should not care to live.

Kārpaṇya-doṣ'opahata-svabhāvaḥ
pṛcchāmi tvāṁ-dharma-saṁmūḍha-
cetāḥ
yac chreyaḥ syān niścitaṁ brūhi tan me

śiṣyas te' haṁ śādhi māṁ tvāṁ
prapannam // 7

My natural disposition is vitiated by a sense of pity, and my mind is in utter confusion regarding my duty. Lord, I beg Thee: tell me with certainty what will lead to my good. I am Thy disciple. Instruct me, who have taken refuge in Thee.

na hi prapaśyāmi mam'āpanudyād
yac chokam ucchoṣaṇam
indriyāṇām /
avāpya bhūmāu asapatnaṁ ṛddhaṁ
rājyaṁ surāṇām api
c'ādhipatyam // 8

I do not find anything that can assuage this grief which numbs my senses. Neither the unchallenged lordship over a prosperous kingdom, nor even the overlordship of all the Devas can do so.

Sañjaya uvāca:

Evam uktvā hṛṣīkeśaṁ
guḍākeśaḥ paraṁtapaḥ /
na yotsya iti Govindam
uktvā tūṣṇīṁ babhūva ha // 9

Sañjaya said:

Addressing Śrī Kṛṣṇa, the master of the senses, Arjuna, though valorous and vigilant, said, 'I will not fight' and sat silent.

Tam uvāca hṛṣīkeśaḥ
Prahasann iva Bhārata /
senayor ubhayor madhye
viṣīdantam idaṁ vacaḥ // 10

O King! To him who was thus sitting grief-stricken between the two armies (instead of fighting), Śrī Kṛṣṇa said as if by way of ridicule.

Śrī bhagavān uvāca
aśocyān anvaśocas tvaṁ
prajñā-vādāṁś ca bhāṣase /
gat'āsūn agat'āsūṁś ca
n'ānuśocanti paṇḍitāḥ // 11

The Blessed Lord said:

You are moaning for those who should not be moaned for. Yet you speak like a wise man. The truly wise never weep either for the dead or for the living.

Na tv'ev'āhaṁ jātu nāsaṁ
na tvaṁ n' eme jan' ādhipāḥ /
na c'aiva na bhaviṣyāmaḥ
sarve vayam ataḥ param // 12

Never was there a time when I did not exist, nor you, nor these rulers of men. Nor shall all of us cease to be hereafter.

Dehino' smin yathā dehe
kaumāraṁ yauvanaṁ jarā /
tathā dehā'ntara prāptir-
dhīras tatra na muhyati // 13

Even as the attainment of childhood, youth and old age is to one in this physical life, so is the change to another body (at death) for the embodied soul. Wise men are not deluded by this.

Mātrā-sparśās tu Kaunteya
śīt'oṣṇa- sukha-duḥkhadāḥ /
āgam'āpāyino'nityāḥ
tāṁs titikṣasva Bhārata // 14

Contact of the senses with their objects generates cold and heat, pleasure and pain. They come and go, being impermanent. Bear with them patiently, O scion of the Bharata race!

Yaṁ hi na vyathayanty ete
puruṣaṁ puruṣ' arṣabha /
sama-duḥkha-sukhaṁ dhīraṁ
so'mṛtatvāya kalpate // 15

O leader of men! That enlightened one who is unpertubed alike in pleasure and pain, whom these do not distress — he indeed is worthy of immortality.

N'āsato vidyate bhāvo
n'ābhāvo vidyate sataḥ /
ubhayor api dṛṣṭo'ntas-
tv anayos tattva darśibhiḥ // 16

The unreal can never come into existence, and the real can never cease to be. The wise philosophers have known the truth about these categories (of the real and the unreal).

Avināśi tu tad viddhi
yena sarvam idaṁ tatam /
vināśam avyayasy'āsya
na kaścit kartum arhati // 17

Know that Reality, by which everything is pervaded, to be indestructible. No one can cause the destruction of this immutable Being.

Antavanta ime dehā
nityasyo'ktāḥ śarīriṇaḥ /

anāśino'prameyasya
tasmād yudhyasva Bhārata // 18

What is said to perish are these bodies, in which the imperishable and unlimited Spirit is embodied. Therefore fight, O scion of the Bharata race!

Ya enaṁ vetti hantāraṁ
yaś c'ainaṁ manyate hatam /
ubhau tau na vijānīto
nāyaṁ hanti na hanyate // 19

He who thinks him (the Self) to be the killer, and who experiences him (the Self) as the killed — both of them know not. He (the Self) neither kills nor is killed.

Na jāyate mriyate vā kadācin-
nāyaṁ bhūtvā bhavitā va nā bhūyaḥ /
ajo nityaḥ śāśvato'yaṁ purāṇo
na hanyate hanyamāne śarīre // 20

He (this Self) has neither birth nor death. Nor does he cease to be, having been in existence before; unborn, eternal permanent and primeval, he is never killed when the body is killed.

Ved'āvināśinaṁ nityaṁ
ya enaṁ ajam avyayam /
kathaṁ sa puruṣaḥ Pārtha
kaṁ ghātayati hanti kam // 21

O Arjuna! know this self to be eternal, undecaying, birthless and indestructible. A person who knows him to be so — whom can he slay or cause another to slay.

Vāsāṁsi jīrṇāni yathā vihāya
navāni gṛhṇāti naro'parāṇi
tathā śarīrāṇi vihāya jīrṇāny-
anyāni saṁyāti navāni dehī // 22

Just as a man gives up old garments and puts on new ones, so the embodied self abandons decrepit bodies and assumes new ones.

Nainaṁ chindanti śastrāṇi
nainaṁ dahati pāvakaḥ /
na c'ainaṁ kledayanty āpo
na śoṣayati mārutaḥ // 23

Him the weapons cleave not; Him the fire burns not; Him the waters wet not; Him the wind dries not.

Acchedyo'yam adāhyo'yam
akledyo'śoṣya eva ca /
nityaḥ sarvagataḥ sthāṇuḥ
acalo'yaṁ sanātanaḥ // 24

He cannot be cut or burnt. He can neither be wetted nor dried. Eternal, all-pervading, immovable and motionless, He is the same for ever.

Avyakto'yaṁ acintyo'yam
avikāryo'yam ucyate /
tasmād evaṁ viditv' ainaṁ
n'ānuśocitum arhasi // 25

Knowing Him (the Self) to be unmanifest, inconceivable, and unmodifiable, it is improper to mourn for Him.

Atha c'ainaṁ nitya-jātaṁ
nityaṁ vā manyase mṛtam /
tathāpi tvaṁ mahā-bāho
n'ainaṁ śocitum arhasi // 26

In the alternative, even if you hold him (the Self) to be subject to constant births and deaths, there is no justification, O mighty armed, for your mourning for him.

Jātasya hi dhruvo mṛtyuḥ
dhruvaṁ janma mṛtasya ca /

tasmād aparihārye'rthe
na tvaṁ śocitum arhasi // 27

For the born, death is unavoidable; and for the dead, birth is sure to take place. Therefore in a situation that is inevitable, there is no justification for you to grieve.

Avyakt'ādīni bhūtāni
vyakta-madhyāni Bhārata /
avyakta-nidhanāny eva
tatra kā paridevanā // 28

Mystery surrounds the origin of beings. Mysterious too is their end. Only in the interim, between birth and death, are they manifested clearly.

Such being the case, what is there to grieve about?

Āścaryavat paśyati kaścit enam
āścaryavad vadati tath'aiva c'ānyaḥ
āścaryavad c'ainam anyaḥ śṛṇoti
śrutvā'py enaṁ veda na c'aiva
kaścit // 29

Some have a glimpse of Him as a marvel, some speak of Him as a marvel, and yet others hear of Him as a marvel. Yet none understands Him in truth, in spite of (seeing, speaking and) hearing about Him.

Dehī nityam avadhyo'yaṁ
dehe sarvasya Bhārata

tasmāt sarvāṇi bhūtāni
na tvaṁ śocitum arhasi // 30

At no time can the Spirit embodied in all beings be slain. Therefore there is no reason for you to grieve for any one.

Svadharmam api c'āvekṣya
na vikaṁpitum arhasi
dharmyād dhi yuddācchreyo'nyat
kṣatriyasya na vidyate // 31

Further, even from the point of view of one's own duty, you ought not to falter. There is no greater good for a Kṣatriya than what a righteous war offers.

Yadṛcchayā c'opapannaṁ
svarga-dvāram apāvṛtam /
sukhinaḥ kṣatriyāḥ Pārtha
labhante yuddham īdṛśam // 32

O Arjuna! That Kṣatriya must indeed be a happy man to whom comes unsought a war like this, which is an open gate to heaven.

Atha cet tvam imaṁ dharmyaṁ
saṅgrāmaṁ na kariṣyasi /
tataḥ svadharmaṁ kīrtiṁ ca
hitvā pāpam avāpsyasi // 33

If you do not take part in this righteous war, you will incur sin, besides failing in your duty and forfeiting your reputation.

Akīrtiṁ c'āpi bhūtāni
kathayiṣyanti te'vyayām /
sambhāvitasya cākīrtir-
maraṇād atiricyate // 34

Besides, every one will speak ill of you for all time. More poignant than death is disrepute to a man accustomed to be honoured by all.

Bhayād raṇād uparataṁ
maṁsyante tvāṁ mahā-rathāḥ /
yeṣāṁ ca tvaṁ bahumato
bhūtvā yāsyasi lāghavam // 35

The great car-warriors will consider you as having fled from battle out of fear, and you who have been the object of their respect, will be despised by them hereafter.

Avācya-vādāṁś ca bahūn
vadiṣyanti tav' āhitāḥ
nindantas tava sāmarthyaṁ
tato duḥkhataraṁ nu kim // 36

Your enemies will indulge in derogatory speeches against you, belittling your prowess. What is more painful than that?

Hato vā prāpsyasi svargaṁ
jitvā vā bhokṣyase mahīm /
tasmād uttiṣṭha Kaunteya
yuddhāya kṛta-niścayaḥ // 37

O son of Kunti! If killed in battle you will attain heaven; if victorious you will enjoy the kingdom. Therefore arise, resolved to fight.

sukha-duḥkhe same kṛtvā
lābh'ālābhau jay'ājayau /
tato yuddhāya yujyasva
n'aivaṁ pāpam avāpsyasi // 38

Treating alike pleasure and pain, gain and loss, victory and defeat, be ready for battle. Thus you will not incur any sin.

Eṣā te'bhihitā sāṁkhye
buddhir yoge tvimāṁ śṛṇu
buddhyā yukto yayā Pārtha
karma-bandhaṁ prahāsyasi 39

O Arjuna! What has been declared to you is the Truth according to the Sāṁkhya (the path of knowledge). Listen now to the teaching of Yoga (the path of selfless action combined with devotion) by practising which the bondage of Karma is overcome.

n' eh'ābhikrama-nāśo'sti
pratyavāyo na vidyate /
svalpam apy asya dharmasya
trāyate mahato bhayāt // 40

In this path of Yoga — the path of selfless action combined with devotion — no effort is lost due to incompleteness and no contrary effect of an adverse nature is produced due to failures. Even a little observance of this discipline saves one from great fear.

Vyavasāy'ātmikā buddhir
ek'eha Kuru-nandana
bahu-śākhā hy anantāś-ca
buddhayo' vyavasāyinām // 41

O Arjuna! In those following this path, the Buddhi (the understanding) that has the nature of producing conviction, is directed towards a single objective. In those without any spiritual conviction, the understanding gets scattered and pursues countless ends.

Yām imāṁ puṣpitāṁ vācaṁ
pravadanty avipaścitaḥ /
vedavāda-ratāḥ Pārtha
nānyad ast'īti vādinaḥ //

Kām'ātmānaḥ svarga-parāḥ
janma-karma-phalapradām /
kriyā-viśeṣa-bahulāṁ
bhog'aiśvarya-gatiṁ prati //

Bhog'aiśvarya-prasaktānāṁ
tay'āpahṛta-cetasām /
vyavasāy'ātmikā buddhiḥ
samādhau na vidhīyate // 42-44

O Arjuna! There are people who delight in the eulogistic statements of the Vedas and argue that the purport of the Vedas consists in these and nothing else. They are full of worldly desires; paradise is their highest goal; and they are totally blind in a spiritual sense. They expatiate upon those florid Vedic texts which describe the means for the attainment of pleasure and power, which provide attractive embodiments as the fruits of actions and which are full of descriptions of rites and rituals (through which these fulfilments are obtained). In the minds of these votaries of pleasure and power, addicted to enjoyments of the above description, steadfast wisdom (capable of revealing the Truth) is never generated.

Traiguṇya viṣayā vedā
nistraiguṇyo bhav'ārjuna /
nirdvandvo nitya-sattvastho
niryogakṣema ātmavān // 45

O Arjuna! The Vedas deal with material ends. But you be established in the Spirit, in the immutable purity of it, having abandoned all material values, attachment to possessions, and concern with the contraries of life like pleasure and pain, heat and cold.

Yāvān artha udapāne
sarvataḥ saṁplut' odake /
tāvān sarveṣu vedeṣu
brāhmaṇasya vijānataḥ // 46

What use a pond has got when a whole country is flooded, that much of use only the Veda has got to a Brāhmaṇa who is full of wisdom.

Karmaṇy ev'ādhikāras te
mā phaleṣu kadācana /
mā karma-phala-hetur bhūr-
mā te sango'stv akarmaṇi // 47

To work alone you have competence, and not to claim their fruits. Let not the longing for fruits be the motive force of your action. At the same time let not this attitude confirm you in indolent inaction.

Yogasthaḥ kuru karmāṇi
saṅgaṁ tyaktvā dhanañjayā /

siddhy-asiddhyoḥ samo bhūtvā
samatvaṁ yogā ucyate // 48

Engage yourself in action with the mind steadfast in Yoga. Abandon attachments, O Arjuna, and be unperturbed in success and failure. This unperturbed sameness in all conditions is Yoga.

Dūreṇa hy avaraṁ karma
buddhi-yogād dhanañjaya /
buddhau śaraṇam anviccha
kṛpaṇāḥ phala-hetavaḥ // 49

O Arjuna, mere action (with attachment) is far inferior to action done with the mind poised in evenness. Seek shelter in this state of unperturbed evenness (which can arise only in a desireless mind in communion with the Divine). Those who work for selfish gains are indeed pitiable.

Buddhi-yukto jahatī ha
ubhe sukṛta-duṣkṛte /
tasmād yogāya yujyasva
yogaḥ karmasu kauśalam // 50

One endowed with this unperturbed evenness of mind abandons the effects of both good and bad actions even here itself. Therefore strive for this state of Yoga. Yoga is skill in action.

Karmajaṁ buddhi-yuktā hi
phalaṁ tyaktvā manīṣiṇaḥ /
janma-bandha-vinirmuktāḥ
padaṁ gacchanty anāmayam // 51

Wise men, established thus in the unperturbed evenness of mind, abandon the fruits of action, free themselves from entanglement in the cycle of births and deaths, and attain to the state of freedom from all sorrow (liberation).

Yadā te moha-kalilaṁ
buddhir vyatitariṣyati /
tadā gantā'si nirvedaṁ
śrotavyasya śrutasya ca // 52

When you have overcome the delusions of your understanding sprung from self-centred attachment, then you attain to a state of indifference towards all the past experiences and the others yet to be had.

Śruti-vipratipannā te
yadā sthāsyati niścalā /
samādhāv acalā buddhiḥ
tadā yogam avāpsyasi // 53

When your intellect, fed up with the bewildering scriptural doctrines and their interpretations, settles (finally) in steady and unwavering introspection, then you will attain to real Yoga.

Arjuna uvāca:

Sthita-prajñasya kā bhāṣā
samādhi-sthasya Keśava
sthita-dhīḥ kiṁ prabhāṣeta
kim āsīta vrajeta kim // 54

Arjuna said:

O Kesava! What are the signs of a person who has attained to steady wisdom and deep introspection? How does he speak? How does he sit? How does he walk? (How does he behave in life generally?)

Śrī Bhagavān uvāca:

Prajahāti yadā kāmān
sarvān Pārtha mano-gatān /

ātmany-evā'tmanā tuṣṭaḥ
sthita-prajñas tado'cyate // 55

The Blessed Lord said:

O Son of Pṛthā! When all the desires of the heart have been abandoned, and the Spirit finds joyous satisfaction in Itself (without dependence on any external factor) — then is one spoken of as a person of steady wisdom.

Duḥkheṣv anudvigna-manāḥ
sukheṣu vigata-spṛhaḥ /
vīta-rāga-bhaya-krodhaḥ
sthita-dhīr munir ucyate // 56

Whose mind is not agitated in adversity, who is free from desire, and who is devoid of attachments, fear and anger — such a person is called a sage of steady wisdom.

Yaḥ sarvatr'ānabhisnehas
tat-tat prāpya śubh'āśubham /
n'ābhinandati na dveṣti
tasya prajñā pratiṣṭhitā // 57

Whoever is without self-centred affection for anything, who rejoices not in favourable situations and hates not in unfavourable ones — such a person's wisdom is firmly set.

Yadā saṁharate cāyaṁ
kūrmo'ṅgānī'va sarvaśaḥ /
indriyāṇī'ndriyārthebhyas-
tasya prajñā pratiṣṭhitā // 58

When a person can withdraw his senses from their objects just like the tortoise its limbs on all sides, his wisdom is firmly set.

Viṣayā vinivartante
nirāhārasya dehinaḥ /
rasa-varjaṁ raso'py asya
paraṁ dṛṣṭvā nivartate // 59

From the abstinent soul sense objects fall away, but not the taste for them. When the Supreme Truth is realised, even the taste departs.

Yatato hy api Kaunteya
puruṣasya vipaścitaḥ /
indriyāṇi pramāthīni
haranti prasabhaṁ manaḥ // 60

O son of Kunti! The turbulent senses do violently draw away the mind of even a discerning person who is earnestly striving on the spiritual path.

Tāni sarvāni saṁyamya
yukta āsīta mat-paraḥ /
vaśe hi yaśy'endriyāṇi
tasya prajñā pratiṣṭhitā // 61

Having controlled them all, one should become entirely devoted to Me. He whose senses are under control, his wisdom is firmly set.

Dhyāyato viṣayān puṁsaḥ
saṅgās teụsu'pajāyate /

saṅgāt saṁjāyate kāmaḥ
kāmāt krodho' bhijāyate // 62

In one who dwells longingly on sense objects, an inclination towards them is generated. This inclination develops into desire, and desire begets anger.

Krodhād bhavati saṁmohaḥ
saṁmohāt smṛti-vibhramaḥ /
smṛti-bhraṁśād buddhi-nāśo
buddhi-nāśāt praṇaśyati // 63

Anger generates delusion, and delusion results in loss of memory. Loss of memory brings about the destruction of discriminative intelligence, and loss of discriminative intelligence spells ruin to a man.

Rāga-dveṣa-viyuktais tu
viṣayān indriyaiś caran /
ātma-vaśyair vidhey'ātmā
prasādam adhigacchati // 64

A man of disciplined mind, who has his senses under control and who has neither attraction nor aversion for sense objects, attains tranquillity, though he may be moving amidst objects of the senses.

Prasāde sarva-duḥkhānāṁ
hānir asyo'pajāyate /
prasanna-cetaso hy āśu
buddhiḥ paryavatiṣṭhate // 65

On attaining tranquillity all one's sorrows come to an end. For soon does the intellect of a tranquil person become steady.

Nāsti buddhir ayuktasya
na c'āyuktasya bhāvanā /
na c'ābhāvayataḥ śantir
aśāntasya kutaḥ sukham // 66

A man of uncontrolled senses has no spiritual comprehension. He has no capacity for meditation either. For the unmeditative there is no peace. And where is happiness for one without peace of mind?

Indriyāṇāṁ hi caratāṁ
yan mano' nuvidhīyate /

tad asya harati prajñāṁ
vāyur nāvām ivāmbhasi // 67

The senses are naturally disposed to move towards their objects. Whichever of these senses the mind pursues, that sense carries away that mind as a gale does a ship on the high seas.

Tasmād yasya mahā-bāho
nigṛhītāni sarvaśaḥ /
indriyāṇ'īndriy'ārthebhyas-
tasya prajñā pratiṣṭhitā // 68

Therefore, O mighty Arjuna, he who can completely restrain his senses from pursuing their objects, has his wisdom firmly set.

Yā niśā sarva-bhūtānāṁ
tasyāṁ jāgarti saṁyamī /
yasyāṁ jāgrati bhūtāni
sā niśā paśyato muneḥ // 69

What is like night to all ignorant beings, to that Atman consciousness the self-controlled sage is awake; and the sensate life to which all ignorant beings are awake, that is like night to this illumined sage.

Āpūryamāṇam acala-pratiṣṭhaṁ
samudram āpaḥ praviśanti yadvat /
tadvat kāmā yaṁ praviśanti sarve
sa śāntim āpnoti na kāma-kāmī // 70

He into whom objects of desire enter (unsought and causing no perturbation), even like the ocean that is ever being filled by the rivers but still remains steady within its bounds — such a person attains to peace, not he who runs madly after objects of desire.

Vihāya kāmān yaḥ sarvān
pumāṁs carati niḥspṛhaḥ /
nirmamo nirahaṁkāraḥ
sa śāntim adhigacchati // 71

Whoever has abandoned desires, and moves about without attachments and the sense of 'I' and 'mine' — he attains to peace.

Eṣā brāhmī sthitiḥ Pārtha
n'aināṁ prāpya vimuhyati /

sthitvā'syām antakāle' pi
brahma-nirvāṇam ṛcchati // 72

This, O son of Pṛthā, is the state of dwelling in Brahman. Having attained it, one is no more deluded. By abiding in that state even by the time of death, one is united with Brahman.

Chapter III

Yoga of Action

Arjuna uvāca:

Jyāyasī cet karmaṇas te
matā buddhir, Janārdana /
tat kiṁ karmaṇi ghore māṁ
niyojayasi, Keśava // 1

Arjuna said:

O Janārdana, if, according to Thee, discriminative insight is superior to action, why dost Thou enjoin on me this terrible action (of engagement in war)?

Vyāmiśreṇeva vākyena
buddhiṁ mohayasīva me /
tad ekaṁ vada niścitya
yena śreyo'ham āpnuyām // 2

By seemingly conflicting words, Thou art confusing my understanding. Speak to me only about that which will definitely lead to my highest good.

Śrī Bhagavān uvāca:

Loke'smin dvividhā niṣṭhā
purā proktā mayā'nagha /
jñāna yogena sāṁkhyānāṁ
karma yogena yoginām // 3

The Blessed Lord said:

In times of yore a twofold spiritual path was taught by me, O sinless one — that of knowledge for Sāṁkhyas (who are pure contemplatives), and that of action for Yogis (who combine detached work with devotion).

Na karmaṇām anārambhān-
naiṣkarmyaṁ puruṣo' śnute /
na ca saṁnyasanād eva
siddhiṁ samadhigacchati // 4

By non-performance of action a man does not gain the state of spiritual passivity (or the state of egoless actionlessness called Naiṣkarmya). By mere external abandonment (Saṁnyasa), he does not attain to perfection.

Na hi kaścit kṣaṇam api
jātu tiṣṭhaty akarma-kṛt /
kāryate hy avaśaḥ karma
sarvaḥ prakṛtijair guṇaiḥ // 5

No man can ever remain even for a moment without performing any action. The impulses of nature deprive him of freedom in this respect and compel him to act.

Karm'endriyāni saṁyamya
ya āste manasā smaran /

indriy'ārthān vimūḍhātmā
mithy'ācāraḥ sa ucyate // 6

He who restrains the organs of action but continues to brood in his mind over the objects of sensual desire (enjoyed through them) — such a deluded person is called a hypocrite.

Yas tv indriyāṇi manasā
niyamy'ārabhate'rjuna /
karm-endriyaiḥ karma yogam
asaktaḥ sa viśiṣyate // 7

But he who, controlling all sense organs (by the power of his will) and becoming non-attached, lives a life of communion through dedicated action such a person excels.

Niyataṁ kuru karma tvaṁ
karma jyāyo hy akarmaṇaḥ /
śarīra-yatrā'pi ca te
na prasiddhyed akarmaṇaḥ // 8

Perform your prescribed duties. For, action is superior to inaction. If you are totally inactive, even the survival of the body would become impossible

Yajñ'ārthāt karmaṇo'nyatra
loko'yaṁ karma-bandhanaḥ /
tad-arthaṁ karma Kaunteya
mukta-saṅgaḥ samācara // 9

O son of Kunti! In this world all actions, unless they are done as an offering to God (or as Yajña), become causes of bondage. Therefore, work for the sake of God without personal attachments.

Saha yajñāḥ prajāḥ sṛṣṭvā
puro'vāca Prajāpatiḥ /
anena prasaviṣyadhvam
eṣa vo'stva iṣṭa-kāmadhuk // 10

In the beginning Prajapati, having created men together with Yajña (selfless work dedicated to God or Vedic sacrifice) as their duty, declared: "By this shall you multiply.

May this be to you the Cow of Plenty yielding all your wants!"

Devān bhāvayat' ānena
te devā bhāvayantu vaḥ /
parasparaṁ bhāvayantaḥ
śreyaḥ param avāpsyatha // 11

"You cherish the Devas with Yajña, and may the Devas in turn bless you (with rain and other desired gifts)! Thus, mutually cherishing, you shall attain the highest good.

Iṣṭān bhogān hi vo devā
dāsyante yajña-bhāvitāḥ /
tair dattān apradāy' aibhyo
yo bhuṅkte stena eva saḥ // 12

Worshipped by sacrifices, the Devas will give you the desired objects of enjoyment. They are verily thieves who enjoy their gifts without giving their share in return.

Yajña-śiṣṭ'āśinaḥ santo
mucyante sarva-kilbiṣaiḥ /
bhuñjate te tv aghaṃ pāpā
ye pacanty ātma kāranāt // 13

Those persons who eat what is left after sacrifice, are released from all sin. But those who cook food for the self alone (without sharing it with others), such degraded men eat sin.

Annād bhavanti bhūtāni
parjanyād anna-saṁbhavaḥ /
yajñād bhavati parjanyo
yajñaḥ karma-samudbhavaḥ // 14

From food (i.e., from reproductive power sustained by food) creatures are born. Food is produced by rain. Rain is born of sacrifice, and sacrifice orginates from action.

Karma brahm'odbhavaṁ viddhi
brahmā'kṣara-samudbhavam /
tasmāt sarvagataṁ brahma
nityam yajñe pratiṣṭhitam // 15

Works of sacrifice have their authority in the Veda. Veda has been revealed by the Supreme Being. Therefore the all-comprehending Veda is established in sacrifice (that is, has performance of sacrifice as its fundamental teaching).

Evaṁ pravartitaṁ cakraṁ
n'ānuvartayatī'ha yaḥ /
agh'āyur indriy'ārāmo
moghaṁ Pārtha sa jīvati // 16

Vain is the life of that sinful and sense-indulgent person who fails to fulfil his obligations in this cycle of mutual inter-dependence and service (which the law of sacrifice implies).

Yas tv ātma-ratir eva syād
ātma-tṛptaś ca mānavaḥ /
ātmany eva ca saṁtuṣṭas-
tasya kāryaṁ na vidyate // 17

But whoever delights in the Self (Spirit) alone, and is content and satisfied in the Self, for such a person there is no obligatory duty to discharge.

N'aiva tasya kṛten' ārtho
n'ākṛten' eha kaścana /
na c'āsya sarva-bhūteṣu
kaścid artha-vyapāśrayah // 18

He has no object to gain here in this world by action. Nor does he lose anything by abstaining from action.

For him, there is no dependence on any created being for any object of his.

Tasmād asaktaḥ satataṁ
kāryaṁ karma samācara /
asakto hy ācaran karma
param āpnoti pūruṣaḥ // 19

Therefore perform action always without attachment. For, by working without attachment a man attains the Supreme.

Karmaṇ'aiva hi saṁsiddhim
āsthitā Janakādayaḥ /
loka-saṁgraham evā pi
saṁpaśyan kartum arhasi // 20

Men like Janaka verily attained to perfection by work alone. You ought to work for the good of the world (having their example in view).

Yad-yad ācarati śreṣṭhas-
tat-tad ev'etaro janaḥ /
sa yat pramāṇaṁ kurute
lokas tad anuvartate // 21

Whatever the noblest persons do, the ordinary man imitates. The standard they set, the ordinary men follow.

Na me Pārthā'sti kartavyaṁ
triṣu lokeṣu kiñcana /

n'ānavāptam avāptavyaṁ
varta eva ca karmaṇi // 22

In all the three worlds there is nothing, O son of Pṛtha, that is binding on Me as duty. Neither is there anything that I have to gain, nor anything that I cannot gain. Still I am always engaged in work.

Yadi hy ahaṁ na varteyaṁ
jātu karmaṇy atandritaḥ /
mama vartm'ānuvartante
manuṣyāḥ Pārtha sarvaśaḥ // 23

O son of Pṛtha! If I did not ever continue in action unwearied, men all around would have followed My way.

Utsīdeyur ime lokā
na kuryāṁ karma ced aham /
saṁkarasya ca kartā syām
upahanyām imāḥ prajāḥ // 24

If I were not to work, all these worlds would have perished. I would have been the cause of confusion among men and of their ultimate destruction.

Saktāḥ karmaṇy avidvāṁso
yathā kurvanti Bhārata /
kuryād vidvāṁs tathā'saktaś
cikīrṣur loka-saṁgraham // 25

O scion of the Bharata race! Just as ignorant men do action out of attachment, so let enlightened ones perform the same unattached, with the good of the world in view.

Na buddhi-bhedaṁ janayed
ajñānāṁ karma-saṅginām /
joṣayet sarva-karmāṇi
vidvān yuktaḥ samācaran // 26

An enlightened man should not cause confusion in the minds of ignorant people (by his conduct). Himself working with equanimity, he should make them interested in all activities.

Prakṛteḥ kriyamāṇāni
guṇaiḥ karmāṇi sarvaśaḥ /

ahaṁkāra-vimūḍh'ātmā
kartā'ham iti manyate // 27

Everywhere the dispositions (powers) of Nature perform all works. But deluded by egoism, man thinks, 'I am the doer.'

Tattva-vit tu mahā-bāho
guṇa-karma-vibhāgayoḥ /
guṇā guṇeṣu vartanta
iti matvā na sajjate // 28

But those who know the truth that the dispositions of Nature and the actions which spring from them are distinct from the Self, do not get attached, understanding that it is not the Self, but the dispositions of Nature as organs that settle on the respective objects which too are products of the same dispositions.

Prakṛter guṇa-sammūḍhāḥ
sajjante guṇa-karmasu /
tān akṛtsna-vido mandān
kṛtsna-vin na vicālayet // 29

Men, deluded by the dispositions of Nature, get attached to work prompted by these dispositions. Those who know the whole Truth should not unsettle these dull-witted men of imperfect understanding.

Mayi sarvāṇi karmāṇi
saṁnyasy'adhyātma-cetasā /
nirāśīr nirmamo bhūtvā
yudhyasva vigata-jvaraḥ //30

Offering all your actions to Me, your mind in unison with the spirit and free from desires and egotism, you fight without the slightest touch of hatred or excitement.

Ye me matam idaṁ nityaṁ
anutiṣṭhanti mānavāḥ /
śraddhāvanto'nasūyanto
mucyante te'pi karmabhiḥ // 31

Whoever follow this teaching of mine, with their minds full of faith and free from disparagement, they also are released from the bondage of Karma.

Ye tv etad abhyasūyanto
n'ānutiṣṭhanti me matam /
sarva-jñāna vimūḍhāṁs tān
viddhi naṣṭān acetasaḥ // 32

But those who disparage this doctrine of Mine and discard it, know such senseless men, blind to all wisdom, as lost.

Sadṛśaṁ ceṣṭate svasyāḥ
prakṛter jñānavān api /
prakṛtiṁ yānti bhūtāni
nigrahaḥ kiṁ kariṣyati // 33

Even a wise man acts in accordance with his nature. All beings follow their nature. What can repression do?

Indriyasy'endriyasy'ārthe
rāgadveṣau vyavasthitau /
tayor na vaśam āgacchet
tau hy asya paripanthinau // 34

It is natural for each organ to feel attraction or aversion in respect of objects pertaining to each sense. Do not come under their sway, for they are enemies (of all spiritual aspirants).

Śreyān svadharmo viguṇaḥ
para-dharmāt svanuṣṭhitāt /

svadharme nidhanaṁ śreyaḥ
para-dharmo bhay'āvahaḥ // 35

One's own Dharma (duty), even though not glamorous, is better than duty alien to one's growth (Para-dharmaḥ), however well performed. For even death in doing one's duty leads to one's good, while a duty alien to one's growth is burdened with the fear of downfall.

Arjuna uvāca:

Atha kena prayukto'yaṁ
pāpaṁ carati pūruṣaḥ /
anicchann api Vārṣṇeya
balād iva niyojitaḥ // 36

Arjuna said:

What is that, O scion of the Vṛṣṇi race, prompted by which a man is forced, as it were, to live a sinful life even against his will?

Śrī Bhagavān uvāca:

Kāma eṣa krodha eṣa
rajo-guṇa-samudbhavaḥ /
mah'āśano mahā-pāpmā
viddhy enam iha vairiṇam // 37

The Blessed Lord said:

It is lust, it is anger, born of Rajoguṇa, insatiable and prompting man to great sin. Know this to be the enemy (in man's spiritual life).

Dhumen'āvriyate vahnir
yathā' darśo malena ca /
yath'olben'āvṛto garbhas
tathā ten'edam āvṛtam // 38

As fire is enveloped by smoke, mirror by dust and the embryo by the placenta, so is knowledge overcast by lust.

Āvṛtaṁ jñānam etena
jñānino nitya-vairiṇā /
kāma-rupeṇa Kaunteya
duṣpūreṇ'ānalena ca // 39

Knowledge, O Son of Kunti, is covered up by this eternal foe of the aspirant after knowledge — the insatiable fire of lust.

Indriyāṇi mano buddhir
asy'ādhiṣṭhānam ucyate /
etair vimohayaty eṣa
jñānam āvṛtya dehinam // 40

The senses, the mind and the Buddhi are said to be its seat. With these it veils knowledge and deludes the embodied spirit.

Tasmāt tvam indriyāṇy ādau
niyamya bharatarṣabha /
pāpmānam prajahi hy enaṁ
jñāna-vijñāna-nāśanam // 41

Therefore, O scion of the Bharata race, controlling the senses at the beginning itself, slay this foul enemy, the destroyer of all knowledge and realisation.

Indriyāṇi parāṇy āhur
indriyebhyaḥ paraṁ manaḥ /
manasas tu parā buddhir
yo buddheḥ paratas tu saḥ // 42

The senses are great, they say. Superior to the senses is the mind, and superior even to the mind is the intellect. What is superior even to the intellect is He, the Atman.

Evaṁ buddheḥ paraṁ buddhvā
saṁstabhy'ātmānam-ātmanā /
jahi śatruṁ mahā-bāho
kāma-rūpaṁ durāsadam // 43

Thus knowing Him who is superior even to the Buddhi, and controlling the lower self with the higher, kill that tough enemy in the form of lust, O mighty-armed Arjuna!

Chapter IV

Renunciation of Action in Knowledge

Sri Bhagavān uvāca:

Imaṁ Vivasvate yogaṁ
proktavān aham avyayam /
Vivasvān Manave prāha
Manur Ikṣvākave'bravīt // 1

The Blessed Lord said:

I imparted this immortal Yoga to Vivasvān, Vivasvān to Manu, and Manu to Ikṣvāku.

Evaṁ paraṁparā-prāptam
imaṁ rāja'ṛṣyo viduh /
sa kālen'eha mahatā
yogo naṣṭaḥ Paraṁtapa // 2

O scorcher of foes! This Yoga handed down from teacher to disciple in succession, was known to the Rājarṣis (royal sages). But owing to long lapse of time, it was lost to the world.

Sa evāyaṁ mayā te'dya
yogaḥ proktaḥ purātanaḥ /
bhakto'si me sakhā c'eti
rahasyaṁ hy etad uttamam // 3

You are My devotee and friend — thinking thus, I have today declared to you even that ancient Yoga. For, it is a noble secret (imparted by a teacher only to a worthy disciple).

Arjuna uvāca:

Aparaṁ bhavato janma
paraṁ janma Vivasvataḥ /
katham etad vijānīyāṁ
tvam ādau proktavān iti // 4

Arjuna said:

Thy life-time is later, that of Vivasvān was much earlier. How then am I to understand that Thou didst impart this doctrine to him?

Śrī Bhagavān uvāca:

Bahūni me vyatītāni
janmāni tava c'ārjuna /
tāny ahaṁ veda sarvāṇi
na tvaṁ vettha paraṁtapa // 5

The Blessed Lord said:

O Arjuna! You and I have passed through many births; I remember them all, but you do not, O scorcher of foes!

Ajo'pi sann avyay'ātmā
bhūtānām īśvaro'pi san /
prakṛtiṁ svām adhiṣṭhāya
saṁbhavāmy ātma-māyayā // 6

Though birthless and deathless, and the Lord of all beings as well, yet I (the Eternal Being) take birth by My inherent mysterious Power (*Ātma-māyayā*), employing the pure or Sattva aspect of My material Nature (Prakrti).

Yadā yadā hi dharmasya
glānir bhavati Bhārata /
abhyutthānam adharmasya
tad'ātmānaṁ sṛjāmy aham // 7

Whenever there is decline of Dharma and ascendance of Adharma, then, O scion of the Bharata race! I manifest (incarnate) Myself in a body.

Paritrāṇāya sādhūnāṁ
vināśāya ca duṣkṛtām /
dharma-samsthāpan'ārthāya
sambhavāmi yuge yuge // 8

For the protection of the good, for the destruction of the wicked, and for the establishment of Dharma, I am born from age to age.

Janma karma ca me divyam
evaṁ yo vetti tattvataḥ /
tyaktvā dehaṁ punar-janma
nai'ti mām eti so'rjuna // 9

O Arjuna! He who thus understands the truth about My embodiment and My deeds — he, on abandoning his present body, is not reborn; he attains to Me.

Vīta-rāga-bhaya-krodhā
ṃanmayā mām upāśritāḥ /
bahavo jñāna-tapasā
pūtā mad-bhāvam āgatāḥ // 10

Freed from passion, fear and anger, ever absorbed in My thought, and ever dependent on Me — many have attained to My state, being purified by the fire of knowledge and austerity.

Ye yathā māṁ prapadyante
tāms tath'aiva bhajāmy aham /
mama vartm'ānuvartante
manuṣyāḥ Pārtha sarvaśaḥ // 11

O Pārtha! Whosoever worship Me through whatsoever path, I verily accept and bless them in that way. Men everywhere follow My path.

Kāṅkṣantaḥ karmaṇāṁ siddhiṁ
yajanta iha devatāḥ /
kṣipraṁ hi mānuṣe loke
siddhir bhavati karmajā // 12

In this world those who entertain desire for the fruits of pious works, worship the deities. For, in this world of men such actions bear fruit quickly.

Cāturvarṇyaṁ mayā sṛṣṭaṁ
guṇa-karma-vibhāgaśaḥ /
tasya kartāram api māṁ
viddhy akartāram avyayam // 13

According to the aptitudes resulting from the dispositions of Nature (Guṇas) and from works, the social order of fourfold division has been created by Me. Though I am their originator, know Me to be not an agent but the Spirit unchanging.

Na māṁ karmāṇi limpanti
na me karma-phale spṛhā /
iti māṁ yo'bhijānāti
karmabhir na sa badhyate // 14

Actions do not affect Me. Nor have I any desire for the fruits of action. Whoever knows Me to be so, is not bound by Karma.

Evam jñātvā kṛtaṁ karma
pūrvair api mumukṣubhiḥ /
kuru karm'aiva tasmāt tvaṁ
pūrvaiḥ pūrvataraṁ kṛtam // 15

Knowing thus, the ancient aspirants after liberation performed works. Therefore you too do work as these ancients did from time immemorial.

Kiṁ karma kim akarm'eti
kavayo'py atra mohitāḥ /
tat te karma pravakṣyāmi
yaj jñātvā mokṣyase'śubhāt // 16

What is work and what is 'non-work', is a subject regarding which even the wise are perplexed. I shall therefore speak to you about work, by knowing which one is liberated from evil (or the life of bondage in Saṁsāra).

Karmaṇo hy api boddhavyaṁ
boddhavyaṁ ca vikarmaṇaḥ /
akarmaṇaś ca boddhavyaṁ
gahanā karmaṇo gatiḥ // 17

The truth about the nature of 'beneficial work' has to be understood, as also of 'baneful work' and of 'non-work'. The way of work is difficult indeed to understand.

Karmaṇy akarma yaḥ paśyed
akarmaṇi ca karma yaḥ /

sa buddhimān manuṣyeṣu
sa yuktaḥ kṛtsna-karma-kṛt // 18

He who sees work in 'no work' and 'no work' in work, he is wise among men. Even while doing all work, he remains established in Yoga.

Yasya sarve samārambhāḥ
kāma-saṁkalpa-varjitāḥ /
jñānāgni-dagdha-karmāṇaṁ
tam āhuḥ paṇḍitaṁ budhāḥ // 19

Whose undertakings are devoid of self-centred objectives, whose works have been burnt up by the fire of knowledge — him the wise call a sage.

Tyaktvā karma-phalāsaṅgaṁ
nitya-tṛpto nirāśrayaḥ /
karmaṇy abhipravṛtto'pi
nai'va kiñcit karoti saḥ // 20

Without attachment to the fruits of action, ever-satisfied and free from calculations, he is verily doing nothing, even though engaged in actions.

Nirāśīr yata-citt'ātmā
tyakta-sarva-parigrahaḥ /
śārīraṁ kevalaṁ karma
kurvan n'āpnoti kilbiṣam // 21

One who is free from desires, whose mind is well-controlled, and who is without any sense of ownership, incurs no sin from works, as his actions are merely physical.

Yadṛcchā-lābha-saṁtuṣṭo
dvandv'ātīto vimatsaraḥ /
samaḥ siddhāv asiddhau ca
kṛtvā' pi na nibadhyate // 22

Satisfied with whatever comes without calculations, rising above the contrasting conditions of life, without any competitive spirit, and alike in success and in failure, a man, though working, incurs no sin.

Gata-saṅgasya muktasya
jñān'āvasthita-cetasaḥ /

yajñāy'ācarataḥ karma
samagraṁ pravilīyate // 23

In the case of one who is without attachments and the sense of agency, and whose mind is fully established in the knowledge of God, — his actions, being done in dedication to the Lord, melt away with their very tendencies.

Brahm' ārpaṇaṁ brahma havir-
brahm'āgnau brahmaṇā hutam /
brahm'āiva tena gantavyaṁ
brahma-karma-samādhinā // 24

To one of the above description, the ladle with which the offering is made and the oblations are Brahman; and the sacrificial rite (which is Brahman) is performed by the sacrificer who is Brahman, in the fire which too is Brahman. He who is thus absorbed in work as Brahman, attains to Brahman alone.

Daivam ev'āpare yajñaṁ
yoginaḥ paryupāsate /
brahm'āgnau apare yajñaṁ
yajñen'aiv'opajuhvati // 25

Some Yogis perform sacrifices especially wanting to propitiate deities. Still others offer sacrifice (the Atman) itself as oblation (Yajña) in the fire of Brahman.

Śrotrādīnī 'ndriyāṇy anye
saṁyam'āgniṣu juhvati /
śabdādīn viṣayān anya
indriy'āgniṣu juhvati // 26

Some offer their organs of knowledge like hearing as sacrifice in the fire of restraint, while others take iṇ all their sense perceptions as oblations made in the fire of their respective senses.

Sarvāṇī'ndriya-karmāṇī
prāṇakarmāṇi cā'pare /
ātma-saṁyama yogāgnau
juhvati jñāna-dipite // 27

Others offer all the functions of their senses and vital energy as sacrificial offerings in the fire of self-restraint kindled by knowledge.

Dravya-yajñās tapo-yajñā
yoga-yajñās tathā'pare /
svādhyāya-jñāna-yajñāś ca
yatayaḥ saṁśita-vratāḥ // 28

Likewise others, being of rigid vows and hard practice, offer their wealth, their austerities, their Yogic practices, and their daily study of the Vedas as sacrifice.

Apāne juhvati prāṇaṁ
prāṇe'pāṇaṁ tathā' pare /
prāṅ'āpāna-gatī ruddhvā
prāṇāyāma-parāyaṇāḥ // 29

Others devoted to the practice of Prāṇāyāma, regulate the movement of Prāṇa and Apāna, and offer as oblation Prāṇa in Apāna, and likewise Apāna in Prāṇa.

Apare niyat'āhārāḥ
prāṇān prāṇeṣu juhvati /
sarve'py ete yajña-vido
yajña-kṣapita-kalmaṣāḥ // 30

Some others, who observe regulation of food, make a sacrificial offering of the Prāṇa as the vital energy present in food stuffs, into the prāṇa as the vital energy enlivening the body. All these know the true nature of sacrifice and have all evil in them washed away by Yajña (sacrifice).

Yajña-śiṣṭāmṛta-bhujo
yānti brahma sanātanam /
n'āyam loko'sty ayajñasya
kuto'nyaḥ Kuru-sattama // 31

Those who partake of nectar, the sacramental remnants of sacrifice, attain to the eternal Brahman. O Thou the best of the Kurus! For one who sacrifices not, this world is lost, not to speak then of the hereafter.

Evaṁ bahuvidhā yajñā
vitatā brahmaṇo mukhe /

karmajān viddhi tān sarvān
evaṁ jñātvā vimokṣyase // 32

Thus many forms of sacrifice are set forth prominently in the Vedas (as paths to Brahman). All of them spring from work done by body, mind, and speech. Knowing this, you will attain liberation.

Śreyān dravyamayād yajñāt
jñāna-yajñaḥ Paraṁtapa /
sarvaṁ karmā'khilaṁ Pārtha
jñāne parisamāpyate // 33

O scorcher of enemies! Sacrifice involving knowledge is superior to sacrifice with material objects; for, O son of Pṛthā, all works without exception culminate in knowledge.

Tad viddhi praṇipātena
paripraśnena sevayā /
upadekṣyanti te jñānaṁ
jñāninas tattva-darśinaḥ // 34

With reverential salutations do you approach them — the wise men who have known the Truth. Serve them, and question them repeatedly (with due respect, until your doubts are clarified). These wise men will impart the knowledge of this divine Truth to you.

Yaj jñātvā na punar mohaṁ
evaṁ yāsyasi Pāṇḍava /

yena bhūtāny aśeṣeṇa
drakṣyasy ātmany atho mayi // 35

They will impart to you that divine knowledge by knowing which you will not again fall into such delusion; for you will then see all beings in their entirety in the Self and also in Me.

Api ced asi pāpebhyaḥ
sarvebhyaḥ pāpa-kṛttamaḥ /
sarvaṁ jñāna-plaven'aiva
vṛjinaṁ saṁtariṣyasi // 36

Even if you happen to be the worst of sinners, you will surely go across all sin by the raft of divine knowledge.

Yath'aidhāṁsi samiddho'gnir
bhasmasāt kurute'rjuna /
jñānāgniḥ sarva-karmāṇi
bhasmasāt kurute tathā // 37

Just as a well-kindled fire reduces a heap of fire-wood to ashes, so does the fire of divine knowledge reduce all sins to ashes.

Na hi jñānena sadṛśaṁ
pavitram iha vidyate /
tat svayam yoga-saṁsiddhaḥ
kālen' ātmani vindati // 38

Verily there is nothing so purifying as knowledge in this world. One who is perfect in Yoga discovers it in oneself in course of time.

Śraddhāvāṁ labhate jñānaṁ
tat-paraḥ samyat'endriyaḥ /
jñānaṁ labdhvā parāṁ śāntim
acireṇ'ādhigacchati // 39

A man of deep Faith (Śraddhā) obtains this divine knowledge, being full of zeal and devotion for it and endowed with mastery of the senses. Having obtained that knowledge, he is established in supreme peace very soon.

Ajñaś c'āśraddadhānaś ca
saṁśay'ātmā vinaśyati /

n'āyaṁ loko'sti na paro
na sukhaṁ saṁśay'ātmanaḥ // 40

An ignorant man without any positive faith, who knows only to doubt, goes to ruin. To such a doubting soul there is neither this world nor the world beyond. There is no happiness for him.

Yoga-saṁnyasta-karmāṇaṁ
jñāna-saṁcchinna-saṁśayam /
ātmavantaṁ na karmāṇi
nibadhnanti Dhanañjaya // 41

O Arjuna! Works do not bind one who has abandoned them through Yōga consisting in dedication and detachment, whose doubts have been dispelled by divine knowledge, and who is poised in the Self.

Tasmād ajñāna-saṁbhūtaṁ
hṛt-sthaṁ jñān'āsinā'tmanaḥ /
chittv'ainaṁ saṁśayaṁ yogam
ātiṣṭh'ottiṣṭha Bhārata // 42

Therefore, cutting asunder the sceptical tendency of the heart by the sword of divine knowledge, betake yourself to Yoga (communion through sacrificial action) and arise, O scion of the Bharata race!

Chapter V
Yoga of Renunciation

Arjuna uvāca:

Saṁnyāsam karmaṇāṁ Kṛṣṇa
punar yogaṁ ca śaṁsasi /
yac chreya etayor ekaṁ
tan me brūhi suniścitam // 1

Arjuna said:

O Kṛṣṇa! Thou praisest in one breath both abandonment of works and communion through their performance. Now tell me with certainty which of them leads to one's good.

Śrī Bhagavān uvāca:

Saṁnyāsaḥ karma-yogaś ca
niḥśreyasa-karāv ubhau /
tayos tu karma-samnyāsāt
karma-yogo viśiṣyate // 2

The Blessed Lord said:

Both abandonment of works and communion through works lead to liberation. But of them, communion through work excels abandonment of work.

Jñeyaḥ sa nitya-saṁnyāsī
yo na dveṣṭi na kāṅkṣati /
nirdvandvo hi mahā-bāho
sukhaṁ bandhāt pramucyate // 3

O mighty-armed one! Whoever hates not, nor desires, should be known as one established in renunciation. Indeed, one who is above such contraries is easily liberated from bondage.

Sāṁkhya-yogau pṛthag bālāḥ
pravadanti na paṇḍitāḥ /
ekam apy āsthitaḥ samyag
ubhayor vindate phalam // 4

It is only the childish and not the wise that speak of Sāṁkhya (or Knowledge accompanied by abandonment of work) and Yoga (or communion through detached and dedicated work) as different. A person well-established in even one of these, attains the end that is the common goal of both. (That is, in the means they employ, they look different, but their end or ultimate purpose is identical.)

Yat sāṁkhyaiḥ prāpyate sthānaṁ
tad yogair api gamyate /
ekaṁ sāṁkhyaṁ ca yogaṁ ca
yaḥ paśyati sa paśyati // 5

The state which one attains by Sāṁkhya, that same state is attained by Yoga too. He who sees both Sāṁkhya and Yoga as one, sees indeed.

Saṁnyāsas tu mahā-bāho
duḥkham āptum ayogataḥ /
yoga-yukto munir brahma
nacireṇ'ādhigacchati // 6

O mighty-armed Arjuna! True abandonment of work (which the discipline of Sāṁkhya implies) is difficult to practise for one who is not accomplished in the Yoga discipline of detached work. But the sage accomplished in Yoga attains to Brahman in no long time.

Yoga-yukto viśuddh' ātmā
vijit ātmā jit' endriyaḥ /
sarva-bhūtātma-bhūtātmā
kurvann api na lipyate // 7

One who is established in selfless and detached action, who is pure, whose mind and senses are under control, and whose self is identified with the self of all — he is never bound, though he be engaged in work.

N'aiva kiñcit karomī' ti
yukto manyeta tattva-vit /
paśyan śṛṇvan spṛśan jighran
aśnan gacchan svapan śvasan //

Pralapan visṛjan gṛhṇan
unmiṣan nimiṣann api /
indriyāṇī'ndriyārtheṣu
vartanta iti dhārayan // 8-9

I (the Self) do naught; only the senses are occupied with their objects

— this should be the conviction of one who is detached in action and established in the truth (that he is the Atman), even while seeing, hearing, touching, smelling, eating, walking, sleeping, breathing, conversing, evacuating, holding, and opening and closing the eyes.

Brahmaṇy ādhāya karmāṇi
saṅgaṁ tyaktvā karoti yaḥ /
lipyate na sa pāpena
padma-patram iv'āmbhasā // 10

One who resigns all his actions to Brahma and works without any personal attachments, is not soiled by sin, as a lotus leaf is not wetted by water.

Kāyena manasā buddhyā
kevalair indriyair api /
yoginaḥ karma kurvanti
saṅgaṁ tyaktv'ātmaśuddhaye // 11

For the attainment of mental purity, spiritual aspirants (Yogins) perform action devoid of attachment, with their body, mind, intellect or even merely with the senses.

Yuktaḥ karma-phalaṁ tyaktvā
śāntim āpnoti naiṣṭhikīm /
ayuktaḥ kāma-kāreṇa
phale sakto nibadhyate // 12

By abandoning the fruits of action a man of restrained mind attains to abiding peace. But the one with unrestrained mind, being prompted by desire for the fruits of action, gets bound.

Sarva-karmāṇi manasā
saṁnyasy'āste sukhaṁ vaśī /
nava-dvāre pure dehī
n'aiva kurvan na kārayan // 13

A self-controlled soul, having abandoned all work mentally (in the way described above), resides at ease (as a witness) in this corporeal mansion with nine gates, neither working nor causing work to be done.

Na kartṛtvaṁ na karmāṇi
lokasya sṛjati prabhuḥ /
na karma-phala-saṁyogaṁ
svabhāvas tu pravartate // 14

In regard to all beings in this world, the sovereign soul is not the cause of the sense of agency, nor of actions, nor of the fruition of actions. It is Nature that does all this.

N'ādatte kasyacit pāpaṁ
na c'aiva sukṛtaṁ vibhuḥ /
ajñānen'āvṛtaṁ jñānaṁ
tena muhyanti jantavaḥ // 15

The all-pervading Being does not accept the sins or merits of any one. Knowledge of the Divine Spirit is veiled by ignorance, and therefore beings are deluded.

Jñānena tu tad ajñānaṁ
yeṣāṁ nāśitam ātmanaḥ /
teṣām adityavaj jñānaṁ
prakāśyati tat param // 16

But in the case of those whose ignorance has been destroyed by the knowledge of the Atman, to them that knowledge reveals the supreme Truth, as the sun does the objects of the world.

Tad-buddhayas tad-ātmānas
tan-niṣṭhās tat-parāyaṇāḥ /
gacchanty apunar-āvṛttiṁ
jñāna-nirdhūta-kalmaṣāḥ // 17

Those who think of That always, who are ever at one with That, who are deeply devoted to That, and who look upon That as their goal, get purified of their sins by divine knowledge and go to the state from which there is no return to worldly life.

Vidyā-vinaya-sampanne
brāhmaṇe gavi hastini /
śuni c'aiva śvapāke ca
paṇḍitāḥ sama-darśinaḥ // 18

Enlightened men are those who see the same (i.e. the Atman) in a Brāhmaṇa with learning and humility, in a cow, in an elephant, and even in

—a dog or in an eater of dog-meat (outcaste).

Ih'aiva tair jitaḥ sargo
yeṣāṁ sāmye sthitaṁ manaḥ /
nirdoṣaṁ hi samaṁ brahma
tasmād brahmaṇi te sthitāḥ // 19

Even here in this embodied state, the cycle of births and deaths has been overcome by those who have this vision of sameness in all. Verily, Brahman is the Unsullied and the Pure. Therefore are those seers of sameness said to be established in Brahman.

Na prahṛṣyet priyaṁ prāpya
n'odivijet prāpya cā'priyam /

sthira-buddhir asaṁmūḍho
brahma-vid brahmaṇi sthitaḥ // 20

Unperturbed and undeluded, a knower of Brahman, who is established in Him, neither rejoices at pleasant experiences nor gets agitated at unpleasant ones.

Bāhya-sparśeṣv asakt'ātmā
vindaty ātmani yat sukham /
sa brahma-yoga-yuktātmā
sukham akṣayam aśnute // 21

An aspirant who is unattached to the contactual experiences of the external world, gains the joy that is in the Self within. He enjoys unending bliss with his mind absorbed in communion with Brahman.

Ye hi saṁsparśa-jā bhogā
duḥkha-yonaya eva te /
ādy-anta vantaḥ Kaunteya
na teṣu ramate budhaḥ // 22

Whatever enjoyments are there born of sense contact, they are sources of suffering only. For, they are with a beginning and an end. A wise man finds no delight in them.

Śaknotī h'aiva yaḥ soḍhuṁ
prāk śarīra-vimokṣaṇāt /
kāma-krodh'odbhavaṁ vegam
sa yuktaḥ sa sukhī naraḥ // 23

Here, even while in the body, whoever is able to withstand the agitation caused by lust and anger, he is the self-controlled one, he is the happy man.

Yo'ntaḥ-sukho'ntar-ārāmas
tathāntar-jyotir eva yaḥ /
sa yogī brahma-nirvāṇaṁ
brahma-bhūto'dhigacchati // 24

The Yogin whose happiness is within, whose resting place is within, who likewise experiences the light within — he realises himself to be the Spirit and attains to beatitude in Brahman.

Labhante brahma-nirvāṇaṁ
ṛṣayaḥ kṣīṇa-kalmaṣāḥ /
chinna-dvaidhā yat'ātmānaḥ
sarva-bhūta-hite ratāḥ // 25

Verily, they attain to beatitude in Brahman who are sinless, whose doubts have been destroyed, whose self is under their control and who rejoice in the good of all.

Kāma-krodha-viyuktānāṁ
yatīnāṁ yata-cetasām /
abhito brahma-nirvāṇaṁ
vartate vidit'ātmanām // 26

To those self-controlled ones (ascetics) who are free from lust and anger, who have controlled their minds and who have known their real nature as the spirit — the attainment of beatitude in Brahman is near at hand.

Sparśān kṛtvā bahir bāhyāṁś
cakṣuś c'aiv'āntare bhruvoḥ /
prāṇ'āpaṇau samau kṛtvā
nās'ābhyantara-cāriṇau //

Yat'endriya-mano-buddhir
munir mokṣa-parāyanaḥ /
vigat'ecchā-bhaya-krodho
yaḥ sadā mukta eva saḥ // 27-28

Excluding all sense perceptions; fixing the look between the eye brows; steadying the flow of Prāna (out-going breath) and Apāna (incoming breath) through the nostrils; controlling the senses, mind and intellect; devoid of desires, fear and anger; and aspiring for liberation alone — a meditative sage is liberated for ever.

Bhoktāraṁ yajña-tapasāṁ
sarva-loka-maheśvaram /
suhṛdaṁ sarva-bhūtānāṁ
jñātvā māṁ śāntiṁ ṛcchati // 29

Knowing Me, the recipient of all worship and austere practices, the Supreme Lord of all the worlds, and the friend of all beings, man attains to eternal peace.

Chapter VI
Communion Through Meditation

Śrī Bhagavān uvāca:

Anāśritaḥ karma-phalaṁ
kāryam karma karoti yaḥ /
sa samnyāsī ca yogī ca
na niragnir na c'ākriyaḥ // 1

The Blessed Lord Said:

It is the man who performs his duties without dependence on the fruits that deserves to be called a Sannyāsin (renouncer) and a Yogin, not the one who keeps no fire or aviods works.

Yaṁ saṁnyāsam iti prāhur
yogaṁ taṁ viddhi Pāṇḍava /
na hy asaṁnyasta-saṅkalpo
yogī bhavati kaścana // 2

O son of Pāṇḍu! What is called Sannyāsa or renunciation know that to be identical with Yoga or disciplines of selfless action. For, whoever has not abandoned subtle hankerings and self-centred objectives, can never become a Yogi, or a practitioner of spiritual communion through works.

Ārurukṣor muner yogaṁ
karma kāraṇam ucyate /
yog'ārūḍhasya tsay'aiva
śamaḥ kāraṇam ucyate // 3

For one who desires to ascend the path leading to the heights of spiritual communion (Yoga), detached work is the means. For one who has ascended it, quiescence is verily the means.

Yadā hi n'endriy'ārtheṣu
na karmasv anuṣajjate /
sarva-saṁkalpa-saṁnyāsī
yog'ārūḍhas tad'ocyate // 4

When one ceases to be attached to sense objects and to one's actions, then that one, who has thus abandoned all subtle hankerings and self-centred objectives, is said to have ascended the heights of spiritual communion (Yoga).

Uddhared ātmanā'tmānaṁ
n'ātmānam avasādayet /
ātm'aiva hy ātmano bandhur
atm'aiva ripur ātmanaḥ // 5

One should uplift one's lower self by the higher self. One should not depress or downgrade one's self. For the self verily is both the friend and the foe of the self.

Bandhur ātmā'tmanas tasya
yen'ātm'aiv'ātmanā jitaḥ /
anātmanas tu śatrutve
vartet'ātm'aiva śatruvat // 6

To him who has subdued the lower self by the higher self, the self acts like a friend. But to him who has lost his higher self by the dominance of the lower one, the self functions as the enemy, always hostile to him.

Jit'ātmanaḥ praśāntasya
param'ātmā samāhitaḥ /
śīt'oṣṇa-sukha-duḥkheṣu
tathā mān' āpamānayoḥ // 7

In one who has conquered his mind, the Self remains steady and unperturbed in the experience of the pairs of opposites like heat and cold, pleasure and pain, honour and dishonour.

Jñāna-vijñāna-tṛptātmā
kūṭa-stho vijit'endriyaḥ /

yukta ity ucyate yogī
sama-loṣṭ'āśma-kāñcanaḥ // 8

A Yogin whose spirit has attained contentment through knowledge and experience, who is unperturbed, who has subdued his senses, to whom a lump of earth and a bar of gold are alike — such a Yogi is said to have attained steadfastness in spiritual communion.

Suhṛn-mitr'āry-udāsīna-
madhyastha-dveṣya-bandhuṣu /
sādhuṣv api ca pāpeṣu
sama-buddhir viśiṣyate // 9

Specially noteworthy in excellence is he who is even-minded in his outlook on friend and foe, on comrade and stranger, on the neutral, on the ally, on the good, and even on the evil ones.

Yogī yuñjīta satatam
ātmānaṁ rahasi sthitaḥ /
ekākī yata-citt'ātmā
nirāśīr aparigrahaḥ // 10

Let a Yogin constantly practise spiritual communion, residing alone in a solitary spot, desireless, possessionless, and disciplined in body and mind.

Śucau deśe pratiṣṭhāpya
sthiram āsanam ātmanaḥ /

n'ātyucchritaṁ n'ātinīcaṁ
cail'ājina-kuśottaram //

Tatr'aikāgraṁ manaḥ kṛtvā
yata-citt'endriya-kriyaḥ /
upaviśy'āsane yuñjyād
yogam ātma-viśuddhaye // 11-12

At a clean spot, which is neither too high nor too low, a seat should be made with Kusa grass, spread over with a skin and a cloth. Firmly seated on it, the Yogi should practise spiritual communion, with mind concentrated and with the working of the imaginative faculty and the senses under control, for self-purification.

Samaṁ kāya-śiro-grīvaṁ
dhārayann acalaṁ sthiraḥ /
saṁprekṣya nāsik'āgraṁ svaṁ
diśaś c'ānavalokayan //

Praśāntātmā vigatabhīr
brahmacāri-vrate sthitaḥ /
manaḥ saṁyamya maccitto
yukta āsita matparaḥ // 13-14

Holding the body, head and neck erect, motionless and firm, gazing at the tip of the nose and not round about, fearless, serene, restrained in mind, and established in the vow of continence, he should sit in spiritual communion with Me, looking upon

Me as his highest and most precious end.

Yuñjann evaṁ sadā'tmānaṁ
yogī niyata-mānasaḥ /
śāntiṁ nirvāṇa-paramāṁ
mat-saṁsthām adhigacchati // 15

With the mind restrained from going outward to objects and always uniting with the Supreme in spiritual communion, the Yogi attains to Peace, which is the summit of bliss and enduring establishment in My state.

N'ātyaśnatas tu yogo'sti
na c'aikāntam anaśnataḥ /

na c'āti-svapna-śīlasya
jāgrato n'aiva c'ārjuna // 16

O Arjuna! Success in Yoga is not for those who eat too much, nor for those who eat too little. It is not also for those given to too much sleeping, nor to those who keep vigil too long.

Yukt'āhara-vihārasya
yukta-ceṣṭasya karmasu /
yukta-svapn'-āvabodhasya
yogo bhavati duḥkha-hā // 17

For one who is temperate in food and recreation, who is detached and self-restrained in work, who is regulated in sleep and in vigil — Yoga brings about the cessation of the travail of Samsara.

Yadā viniyataṁ cittam
atmany ev'āvatiṣṭhate /
niḥspṛhaḥ sarva-kāmebhyo
yukta ity ucyate tadā // 18

When the disciplined mind is able to remain established in the Atman alone, when it is free from longing for all objects of desire — then is it spoken of as having attained to spiritual communion.

Yathā dīpo nivāta-stho
n'eṅgate s'opamā smṛtā /
yogino yata-cittasya
yuñjato yogam ātmanaḥ // 19

The flame of a lamp sheltered from wind does not flicker. This is the comparison used to describe a Yogi's mind that is well under control and united with the Ātman.

Yatr'oparamate cittaṁ
niruddhaṁ yoga-sevayā /
yatra c'aiv'ātmanā'tmānaṁ
paśyann ātmani tuṣyati // 20

That state in which the Chitta (mind stuff), with its movements restrained by the practice of Yoga, finds rest; in which is experienced the joy of the Spirit born of the higher mind intuiting the Spirit.

Sukham ātyantikaṁ yat tad
buddhi-grāhyam atīndriyam /
vetti yatra na c'aiv'āyaṁ
sthitaś calati tattvataḥ // 21

In which he (the Yogin) experiences that endless bliss which is beyond the ken of the senses but is intuited by the purified intellect; wherein established, one does not waver from the Truth:

Yaṁ labdhvā c'āparaṁ lābhaṁ
manyate n'ādhikaṁ tataḥ /
yasmin sthito na duḥkhena
guruṇā'pi vicālyate // 22

Having obtained which no other gain is considered as greater; remaining in which one is not shaken even by the heaviest of afflictions,

Taṁ vidyād duḥkha-saṁyoga-
viyogaṁ yoga-saṁjñitam /
sa niścayena yoktavyo
yogo'nirviṇṇa-cetasā // 23

Know that severence of connection with pain as what is designated as Yoga. It has to be practised tirelessly with determination.

Saṁkalpa-prabhavān kāmāṁs
tyaktvā sarvān aśeṣataḥ /

manas'aiv'endriya-grāmaṁ
viniyamya samantataḥ //

Śanaiḥ-śanair uparamed
buddhyā dhṛti-gṛhītayā /
ātma-saṁsthaṁ manaḥ kṛtvā
na kiñcid api cintayet // 24-25

Abandoning imagination - born longings in their entirety, restraining all the senses with the mind on every side, and setting that mind firmly on the Self under the direction of a steadfast intellect, one should practise tranquillity little by little, and abstain from every kind of thought.

Yato-yato niścarati
manaś cañcalam asthiram /

tatas-tato niyamy'aitad
ātmany eva vaśaṁ nayet // 26

From whatsoever reason this wavering and fickle mind wanders away, it should be curbed and brought to abide in the Self alone.

Praśānta-manasaṁ hy enaṁ
yoginaṁ sukham uttamam /
upaiti śānta-rajasaṁ
brahma-bhūtam akalmaṣam // 27

Supreme Bliss wells up in a Yogi, who is tranquil in mind, whose passions are subdued, who is free from impurities and who is in the Brahmic state.

Yuñjann evaṁ sadā'tmānaṁ
yogī vigata-kalmaṣaḥ /
sukhena brahma-saṁsparśam
atyantaṁ sukham aśnute //

Thus, ever engaged in making the mind steadfast in spiritual communion and having all the impurities of the mind effaced thereby, the Yogin easily experiences the infinite Bliss of contact with Brahman.

Sarva-bhūta-stham ātmānaṁ
sarva-bhūtāni c'atmani /
īkṣate yoga-yukt'ātmā
sarvatra sama-darśanaḥ // 29

The man of spiritual insight, established in same-sightedness, sees the Self as residing in all beings and all beings as resting in the Self.

Yo māṁ paśyati sarvatra
sarvaṁ ca mayi paśyati /
tasy'āhaṁ na praṇaśyāmi
sa ca me na praṇaśyati // 30

He who sees Me in all beings, and all beings in Me — to him I am never lost, nor he to Me.

Sarva-bhūta-sthitaṁ yo māṁ
bhajaty ekatvam āsthitaḥ /
sarvathā vartamano'pi
sa yogī mayi vartate // 31

Established in the unity of all existence, a Yogin who serves Me present in all beings, verily abides in Me, whatever be his mode of life.

Ātm'aupamyena sarvatra
samaṁ paśyati yo'rjuna /
sukhaṁ vā yadi vā duḥkhaṁ
sa yogī paramo mataḥ // 32

O Arjuna! In My view that Yogi is the best who, out of a sense of identity with others on account of the perception of the same Atman in all, feels their joy and suffering as his own.

Arjuna uvāca:

Yo'yaṁ yogas tvayā proktaḥ
sāmyena Madhusūdana /

etasy'āham na paśyāmi
cañcalatvāt sthitiṁ sthirām // 33

Arjuna said:

O Slayer of Madhu! Owing to the fickleness of the mind, I find no way of firm establishment in spiritual communion through equanimity as instructed by you.

Cañcalaṁ hi manaḥ Kṛṣṇa
pramāthi balavad dṛḍham /
tasy'āhaṁ nigraham manye
vāyor iva suduṣkaram // 34

O Kṛṣṇa! Verily, the mind is fickle, turbulent, powerful and unyielding.

To control it, I think, is as difficult as controlling the wind itself.

Śrī Bhagavān uvāca:

Asaṁśayaṁ mahā-bāho,
mano durnigrahaṁ calam /
abhyāsena tu Kaunteya
vairāgyeṇa ca gṛhyate // 35

The Blessed Lord said:

O mighty armed one! Undoubtedly the mind is fickle and difficult to be checked. Yet, O son of Kunti, it can be brought under control by dispassion and spiritual practice.

Asaṁyat'ātmanā yogo
duṣprāpa iti me matiḥ /

vaśy'ātmanā tu yatatā
śakyo'vāptum upāyataḥ // 36

My view is that Yoga is difficult of attainment by men of uncontrolled mind. But for those who have their minds under control, it is possible to attain, if they strive with the proper means.

Arjuna uvāca:
Ayatiḥ śraddhay'opeto
yogāc calita-mānasaḥ /
aprāpya yoga-saṁsiddhiṁ
kāṁ gatiṁ Kṛṣṇa gacchati // 37

Arjuna said:

What, O Kṛṣṇa, is the fate of a man who, though endowed with a firm faith, is not steadfast in his practices owing to distractions, and therefore fails to reach spiritual perfection?

Kaccin n'obhaya-vibhraṣṭas
chinn'ābhram iva naśyati /
apratiṣṭho mahā-bāho
vimūḍho brahmaṇaḥ pathi // 38

O mighty-armed Lord! Bewildered in the path of Brahman, supportless, does he not lose both this world and the next? Does he not perish like a rain-cloud rent asunder?

Etan me samśayaṁ Kṛṣṇa
chettum arhasy aśeṣataḥ /

tvad-anyaḥ samśayasy'āsya
chettā na hy upapadyate // 39

O Kṛṣṇa! My doubt in this respect has yet to be cleared completely. Indeed! I find none better than Thee to be that doubt dispeller.

Śrī Bhagavān uvāca:

Pārtha n'aiveha n'āmutra
vināśas tasya vidyate /
na hi kalyāṇa-kṛt kaścid
durgatiṁ tāta gacchati // 40

The Blessed Lord Said:

O son of Pṛthā! He does not meet with downfall either here in this world or in the hereafter. Know for certain, O dear one, that one who treads the path of virtue never goes the way of evil ones.

Prāpya puṇya-kṛtāṁ lokān
uṣitvā śāśvatīḥ samāḥ /

śucīnāṁ śrīmatāṁ gehe
yoga-bhraṣṭo'bhijāyate // 41

The fallen Yogī goes (after death) to the spheres of the righteous, and after having lived there for unnumbered years, is reborn in this world in a pure and prosperous family.

Athavā yoginām eva
kule bhavati dhīmatām /
etadd hi durlabhataraṁ
loke janma yad īdṛśam // 42

Or he is re-born in a family of men full of wisdom and spirituality. Re-birth under such conditions is passing hard to get in this world.

Tatra taṁ buddhi-saṁyogaṁ
labhate paurvadehikam /
yatate ca tato bhūyaḥ
saṁsiddhau Kuru-nandana // 43

There, O scion of the clan of Kurus! he will regain the spiritual discernment of his previous birth, and then he will strive harder than ever for perfection.

Purv'ābhyāsena ten'aiva
hriyate hy avaśo'pi saḥ /
jijñāsur api yogasya
śabda-brahm'ātivartate // 44

Even if helpless, he will be driven towards the path of Yoga by the force of his previous striving. For even a beginner in the path of Yoga goes above the stage requiring the aid of Vedic ritualism (not to speak then of one who has made some progress in Yoga).

Prayatnād yatamānas tu
yogī saṁśuddha-kilbiṣaḥ /
aneka-janma-saṁsiddhas
tato yāti parāṁ gatim // 45

As for the Yogī striving diligently, he is cleansed of all his sins and gains spiritual perfection after passing through several embodiments. Finally he reaches the highest state (which consists in release from the bondage of the body).

Tapasvibhyo'dhiko yogī
jñānibhyo'pi mato'dhikaḥ /
karmibhyaś c'ādhiko yogī
tasmād yogī bhav'ārjuna // 46

A Yogī (one practising meditation) is superior to a man of austerity; he is superior to a scholar; he is superior to a ritualist too. Therefore, O Arjuna, be you a Yogī.

Yoginām api sarveṣāṁ
mad-gaten'āntarātmanā /
śraddhāvān bhajate yo māṁ
sa me yuktatamo mataḥ // 47

Of all the Yogins, he is the most attuned in spiritual communion, who worships Me with abiding faith and with his innermost self fused with Me.

Chapter VII

Communion Through Knowledge

Śrī Bhagavān uvāca:

Mayy āsakta-manāḥ Pārtha
yogaṁ yuñjan mad-āśrayaḥ /
asaṁśayaṁ samagraṁ māṁ
yathājñāsyasi tac chṛṇu // 1

The Blessed Lord said:

Hear now, O son of Pṛthā, how one resigned to Me and absorbed in love of Me, attains to full knowledge of Me through the practice of spiritual communion.

Jñānaṁ te'haṁ savijñānam
idaṁ vakṣyāmy aśeṣataḥ /
yaj jñātvā n'eha bhūyo'nyaj-
jñātavyam avaśiṣyate // 2

I shall now declare to you in fullness that Knowledge along with Special Knowledge, (its higher development), by means of which there will remain nothing more for you to understand.

Manuṣyāṇāṁ sahasreṣu
kaścid yatati siddhaye /
yatatām api siddhānāṁ
kaścin māṁ vetti tattvataḥ // 3

Among thousands of men, there will just be one here or there striving for spiritual perfection. From among the aspirants so striving, one perchance knows Me in truth.

Bhūmir āpo'nalo vāyuḥ
khaṁ mano buddhir eva ca /
ahaṁkāra itī'yaṁ me
bhinnā prakṛtir aṣṭadhā // 4

My Nature is divided into eight categories — earth, water, fire, air, sky, mind, understanding, and I-sense.

Apar'eyam itas tv anyāṁ
prakṛtiṁ viddhi me parām /
jīva-bhūtāṁ mahā-bāho
yay'edaṁ dhāryate jagat // 5

This, O mighty armed, is My lower Nature. Know that, as different from it, is My higher Nature forming the source of all Jivas and the support of the whole universe.

Etad-yonīni bhūtāni
sarvāṇī'ty upadhāraya /
ahaṁ kṛtsnasya jagataḥ
prabhavaḥ pralayas tathā // 6

Know that all beings have these two Natures of Mine as their source. I am the origin and the dissolution of this entire universe.

Mattaḥ parataraṁ n'ānyat
kiñcid asti Dhanañjaya /

mayi sarvam idaṁ protaṁ
sūtre maṇi-gaṇā iva // 7

O Arjuna! There is no being higher than Me. As a row of pearls threaded on a string, all the worlds are held on Me.

Raso'ham apsu Kaunteya
prabhā' smi śaśi-sūryayoḥ /
praṇavaḥ sarva-vedeṣu
śabdaḥ khe pauruṣaṁ nṛṣu // 8

O son of Kunti! In water I am taste; in sun and moon, their brilliance; in all the Vedas, the sound symbol Om; in the sky-element, sound; and in men, their manliness.

Puṇyo gandhaḥ pṛthivyāṁ ca
tejaś c'āsmi vibhāvasau /
jīvanaṁ sarva-bhūteṣu
tapaś c'āsmi tapasviṣu // 9

In the earth element I am sweet fragrance; in fire I am brilliance; in living beings I am the life-principle; and in austere men, I am austerity.

Bījaṁ māṁ sarva-bhūtānāṁ
viddhi Pārtha sanātanam /
buddhir buddhimatām asmi
tejas tejasvinām aham // 10

Know me, O Pārtha! to be the eternal seed of all beings. In the wise I am their wisdom and in puissant men, their prowess.

Balaṁ balavatām cāham
kāma-rāga-vivarjitam
dharm'āviruddho bhūteṣu
kāmo'smi Bharata'rṣabha // 11

In the strong I am strength uncorrupted by desire and attachment, and in living beings I am desire not contrary to virtue.

Ye c'aiva sāttvikā bhāvā
rājasās tāmasāś ca ye /
matta ev'eti tān viddhi
na tv ahaṁ teṣu te mayi // 12

Whatever manifestations there are of Sattva, Rajas and Tamas, they have all come from Me. They are in Me, not I in them.

Tribhir guṇamayair bhāvair
ebhiḥ sarvam idaṁ jagat /
mohitaṁ n'ābhijānāti
mām ebhyaḥ param avyayam // 13

Deluded by the mental states accruing from the three Guṇas of Prakṛti, this world knows not Me, the Imperishable, transcending these Guṇas.

Daivī hy eṣā guṇamayī
mama māyā duratyayā /
mām eva ye prapadyante
māyām etāṁ taranti te // 14

My divine Māyā (power) constituted of the three Guṇas is difficult to overcome. Whoever takes refuge in Me alone, in utter devotion, overcomes it.

Na mām duṣkṛtino mūḍhāḥ
prapadyante nar'ādhamāḥ /
māyayā'pahṛta-jñānā
āsuraṁ bhāvam āśritāḥ // 15

The lowest type of men, evil, foolish and demoniac in nature, being deprived of right understanding by Maya, never take refuge in Me with devotion.

Catur-vidhā bhajante māṁ
janāḥ sukṛtino'rjuna /
ārto jijñāsur arth'ārthī
jñānī ca bharata'rṣabha // 16

O Arjuna, the greatest of the Bharata race! Four kinds of pious men adore Me. They are the distressed one, the knowledge-seeker, the wealth-seeker, and the knower.

Teṣāṁ jñānī nitya-yukta
eka-bhaktir viśiṣyate /
priyo hi jñānino'tyartham
ahaṁ sa ca mama priyaḥ // 17

Among them, the knower (or the man of wisdom), ever communing and single-minded in devotion, is the best. I am indeed supremely dear to such a knower, and he in turn is dear to Me.

Udārāḥ sarva ev'aite
jñānī tv ātm'aiva me mataṁ /
āsthitaḥ sa hi yukt'ātmā
mām ev'ānuttamāṁ gatim // 18

While all of them are certainly noble, the knower I cherish as My very self — such is My view. For, ever in union with Me, he is established in the conviction that I am his highest goal.

Bahūnām janmanām ante
jñānavān māṁ prapadyate /
Vāsudevaḥ sarvam iti
sa mah'ātmā sudurlabhaḥ // 19

At the end of many births (of striving), the knowing one makes Me his refuge, realising that Vasudeva is

All. A great soul of that type is rare to find.

Kāmais tais tair hṛta-jñānāḥ
prapadyante'nya-devatāḥ /
taṁ taṁ niyamam āsthāya
prakṛtyā niyatāḥ svayā // 20

Influenced by their inherent nature and deprived of correct judgement by numerous desires, people adore other deities with various forms of worship pertaining to them.

Yo yo yāṁ yāṁ tanuṁ bhaktaḥ
śraddhayā'rcitum icchati /
tasya-tasy'ācalāṁ śraddhāṁ
tām eva vidadhāmy aham // 21

Whichever devotee desires to adore whatever such Deity with faith, in all such votaries I make that particular faith unshakable.

Sa tayā śraddhayā yuktas
tasy'ārādhanam īhate /
labhate ca tataḥ kāmān
may'aiva vihitān hi tān // 22

Endowed with that faith, a votary performs the worship of that particular deity and obtains the fruits thereof, these being granted by Me alone.

Antavat tu phalaṁ teṣaṁ
tad bhavaty alpa-medhasām /

devān deva-yajo yānti
mad-bhaktā yānti mām api // 23

The results accruing to such small-minded people are finite only. Those who worship the Devas go to the Devas, but My devotees attain to Me.

Avyaktaṁ vyaktim āpannaṁ
manyante mām abuddhayaḥ /
paraṁ bhāvam ajānanto
mamā'vyayam anuttamam // 24

Without any insight into My transcendental nature, unique and immutable, men of little understanding look upon Me as a mere human individual, having come into manifestation from an unmanifested state.

N'āhaṁ prakāśaḥ sarvasya
yoga-māyā samāvṛtaḥ /
mūḍho' yaṁ n'ābhijānāti
loko mām ajam avyayam // 25

Veiled as I am in My Yoga-māyā (Divine Power), I am not revealed to all. This deluded world does not know Me, the unoriginated and the indestructible.

Ved'āhaṁ samatītāni
vartamānāni c'ārjuna /
bhaviṣyāṇi ca bhūtāni
māṁ tu veda na kaścana // 26

O Arjuna! I know all beings — past, present and future. But none knows me.

Icchā-dveṣa-samutthena
dvandva-mohena Bhārata /
sarva-bhutāni saṁmohaṁ
sarge yānti parantapa // 27

O scion of Bharata's house! From their very birth all beings are deluded by the bewitchment of the pairs of opposites like pleasure and pain, springing from the instinctive feelings of attraction and aversion for them.

Yeṣām tv anta-gataṁ pāpaṁ
janānāṁ puṇya-karmaṇām /

te dvandva-moha-nirmuktā
bhajante māṁ dṛḍha-vratāḥ // 28

But those men of virtuous deeds, in whom sinfulness has been effaced — they, freed from the bewilderment of sense life, worship Me with great steadfastness in their vows.

Jarā-maraṇa-mokṣāya
mām āśritya yatanti ye /
te brahma tad viduḥ kṛtsnam
adhyātmaṁ karma c'ākhilam // 29

Those that strive for liberation from the travails of old age and death in complete trust and dependence on Me, shall know all about the Absolute,

His spiritual manifestation and His works of spiritual import.

Sādhibhūt'ādhidaivaṁ māṁ
sādhiyajñaṁ ca ye viduḥ /
prayāṇa-kāle'pi ca māṁ
te vidur yukta-cetasaḥ // 30

Those who have grasped that I am the spiritual power that sustains all material manifestations, all divine expressions and all spiritual endeavours — they continue to know Me as such even at the time of death, their mind being ever absorbed in Me.

Chapter VIII

Way to Brahman

Arjuna uvāca:

Kiṁ tad brahma kim adhyātmaṁ
kim karma puruṣ'ottama /
adhibhūtaṁ ca kiṁ proktam
adhidaivaṁ kiṁ ucyate? // 1

Arjuna said:

O Supreme Lord! What is Brahman (the Absolute)? What is the Spirit (the Adhyātma)? What is work (Karma)? And what is that which underlies the material manifestations (Adhibhūta), and what, the divinities (Adhidaiva)?

Adhiyajñaḥ kathaṁ ko'tra
dehe'smin Madhusūdana /
prayāṇa-kāle ca kathaṁ
jñeyo'si niyat'ātmabhiḥ // 2

O Slayer of Madhu! Who is the Adhiyajña (the spirit underlying sacrifices) that resides in this body, and how does he do so? How should a man of a self-restraint meditate on the Supreme Being at the time of death?

Śrī Bhagavān uvāca:

Akṣaraṁ brahma paramaṁ
svabhāvo'dhyātmam ucyate /
bhūta-bhāvodbhava-karo
visargaḥ karma-samjñitaḥ // 3

The Blessed Lord said:

Brahman is Akṣara, the Immutable Being than whom there is none higher. Brahman's power manifested in every body as the transmigrating self (the Jīva), is the *Adhyātma.* The creative act (identified with sacrificial offering), which brings all beings into existence, is *Karma* (work).

Adhibhūtam kṣaro bhāvaḥ
puruṣaś'c'ādhidaivatam /
adhiyajño'ham ev'ātra
dehe deha-bhṛtāṁ vara // 4

O noble one! The perishable Nature is the material aspect (Adhibhūta).

The cosmic soul is the basis of all divine manifestations (Adhidaivata); and I verily form the Adhiyajña, the one object of all worship which men perform with their body and mind.

Anta-kāle ca mām eva
smaran muktvā kalevaram /
yaḥ prayāti sa mad-bhāvaṁ
yāti n'āsty atra saṁśayaḥ // 5

Whoever thinks of Me alone even at the time of death, attains to My state on abandoning the body. There is no doubt about this.

Yaṁ yaṁ v'āpi smaran bhāvaṁ
tyajaty ante kalevaram /

taṁ tam ev'aiti Kaunteya
sadā tad-bhāva-bhāvitaḥ // 6

O son of Kunti! Whatever object a person thinks of at the time of death, having been absorbed in its thought all through, — he attains to that object alone.

Tasmāt sarveṣu kaleṣu
mām anusmara yudhya ca /
mayy arpita-mano-buddhir
mām ev'aiṣyasy asaṁśayaḥ // 7

Therefore fight, remembering Me always. One who has dedicated his mind and understanding to Me, shall come to Me alone, undoubtedly.

Abhyāsa-yoga-yuktena
cetasā n'ānya-gāminā /
paramaṁ puruṣaṁ divyam
yāti Pārth'ānucintayan // 8

Thinking of Me continuously, with a mind trained in the practice of spiritual communion and freed from the tendency to stray away to other objects, one attains to the Divine Spirit Supreme.

Kaviṁ purāṇam anuśāsitāram
aṇor aṇīyāṁsam anusmared yaḥ /
sarvasya dhātāram acintya-rūpam
āditya-varṇaṁ tamasaḥ parastāt //

Prayāṇa-kāle manasā'calena
bhaktyā yukto yoga-balena c'aiva /

bhruvor madhye prāṇam āveśya samyak
sa taṁ paraṁ puruṣam upaiti divyam // 9-10

He who, with a mind steady and endued with devotion and strength born of spiritual practice, fixes his entire life-force between the eye-brows at the time of death, and contemplates on Him who is all-knowing, primeval, subtler than even an atom, sustainer and director of all, glorious like the sun, and beyond all darkness of inertia and ignorance — he verily attains to that Supreme Being.

Yad akṣaraṁ veda-vido vadanti
viśanti yad yatayo vīta-rāgāḥ /
yad icchanto brahmacaryaṁ caranti
tat te padaṁ saṁgraheṇa
pravakṣye //11

That which Vedic scholars call the Imperishable (Akṣara), which Sannyāsins devoid of worldly attachments enter, desiring which men follow the life of continence and asceticism, — that state I shall declare to you in brief.

Sarva-dvārāṇi saṁyamya
mano hṛdi nirudhya ca /
mūrdhny ādhāy' ātmanaḥ prāṇam
āsthito yoga-dhāraṇām //

Om ity ek'ākṣaraṁ brahma
vyāharan mām anusmaran /
yaḥ prayāti tyajan dehaṁ
sa yāti paramāṁ gatim // 12-13

Established in spiritual communion by inhibiting all sensations, concentrating on the heart centre, and drawing up the vital energies to the head, one should meditate on Me along with the utterance of the single-syllabled mantra Om denoting Brahman. Departing from the body in this state, one attains liberation.

Ananya-cetāḥ satataṁ
yo māṁ smarati nityaśaḥ /

tasy'āhaṁ sulabhaḥ Pārtha
nitya-yuktasya yoginaḥ // 14

He who, with a mind undistracted by other things, thinks of Me constantly every day — to the Yogi thus ever-attuned, I am easy of attainment, O son of Pṛthā!

Mām upetya punar-janma
duḥkh'ālayam aśāśvatam /
n'āpnuvanti mah'ātmānaḥ
saṁsiddhiṁ paramāṁ gatāḥ // 15

No more is re-birth, no more this home of transience and misery, for those great-souled ones who have attained to supreme perfection by realising Me.

Ābrahma-bhuvanāl lokāḥ
punar-āvartino'rjuna /
mām upetya tu Kaunteya
punarjanma na vidyate // 16

All the worlds from the realm of Brahmā down to the earth, are subject to re-birth. But, O Arjuna, one who has attained to Me is never reborn.

Sahasra-yuga-paryantam
ahar yad brahmaṇo viduḥ /
rātriṁ yuga-sahasr'āntāṁ
te'ho-rātra-vido janāḥ // 17

Those who have an understanding of Brahmā's day time, which lasts for a thousand ages, and of his night time, which too is of equal length, — they indeed understand what a day is and what a night.

Avyaktād vyaktayaḥ sarvāḥ
prabhavanty aharāgame /
ratry-āgame pralīyante
tatr'aiv'ā'vyakta saṁjñake // 18

At the dawn of the day of Brahmā this whole universe comes into manifestation from the Unmanifest (Prakṛti). When the night begins, it dissolves in that Unmanifest itself.

Bhūta-grāmaḥ sa ev'āyaṁ
bhūtvā bhūtvā ṗralīyate /
rātry-āgame'vaśaḥ Pārtha
prabhavaty ahar-āgame // 19

O son of Pṛthā! This vast collectivity of beings comes inexorably into manifestation again and again, dissolving at the commencement of night, and again coming forth at the dawn of day.

Paras tasmāt tu bhāvo'nyo'
vyakto'vyaktāt sanātanaḥ /
yaḥ sa sarveṣu bhūteṣu
naśyatsu na vinaśyati // 20

Different from this unmanifested state is the supreme and eternal

Unmanifested whose being remains unaffected even when everything is destroyed.

Avyakto'kṣara ity uktas
tam āhuḥ paramāṁ gatim /
yaṁ prāpya na nivartante
tad dhāma paramaṁ mama // 21

Know that state, which is called the Unmanifested and the Imperishable, to be the ultimate goal of all. That is My supreme abode. Attaining to that, man is not reborn.

Puruṣaḥ sa paraḥ Pārtha
bhaktyā labhyas tv ananyayā /
yasy'āntaḥsthāni bhūtāni
yena sarvam idaṁ tatam // 22

That Supreme Puruṣa, the abode of all beings and the indweller of them all, can be attained by unswerving and exclusive devotion to Him.

Yatra kāle tv anāvṛttiṁ
āvṛttiṁ c'aiva yoginaḥ /
prayātā yānti taṁ kālaṁ /
vakṣyāmi Bharatarṣabha // 23

I shall now tell you, O noblest of Bhāratas, of the circumstances, dying under which a Yogi never returns to this world and also of the time, dying when he is sure to return.

Agnir jyotir ahaḥ śuklaḥ
ṣaṇmāsā uttar'āyaṇam /

tatra prayātā gacchanti
brahma brahma-vido janāḥ // 24

Fire, light, day-time, bright fortnight, six months of the northern course of the sun — the knowers of Brahman who depart along this path, attain to Brahman.

Dhūmo rātris tathā kṛṣṇaḥ
ṣaṇmāsā dakṣiṇ'āyanam /
tatra cāndramasaṁ jyotir
yogī prāpya nivartate // 25

Smoke, night and likewise the black fortnight and the six months of the southern course of the sun — the Yogi departing by this path attains to the lunar sphere and thence returns.

Śukla-kṛṣne gatī hy ete
jagataḥ śāśvate mate /
ekayā yāty anāvṛttim
anyayā'vartate punaḥ // 26

Verily, these two paths — the bright and the dark — are accepted as everlasting verities. By the one, the aspirant gains Mokṣa, the state of non-return, while the other leads him to rebirth.

N'aite sṛtī Pārtha jānan
yogī muhyati kaścana /
tasmāt sarveṣu kāleṣu
yogayukto bhav'ārjuna // 27

O son of Pṛthā! Whoever among Yogis know these two paths, they are never deluded. Therefore, O Arjuna, be steadfast in Yoga at all times.

Vedeṣu yajñeṣu tapaḥsu c'aiva
dāneṣu yat puṇya-phalaṁ pradiṣṭam /
atyeti tat sarvam idaṁ viditvā
yogī paraṁ sthānam upaiti
c'ādyam // 28

Knowing this, a Yogi transcends all the meritorious rewards that are prescribed for the study of the Vedas, for the performance of austerities, and for charities too, and attains to that primeval state, which is the Supreme Being.

Chapter IX

Sovereign Secret

Śrī Bhagavān uvāca:

Idaṁ tu te guhyatamaṁ
pravakṣvāmy anasūyave /
jñānaṁ vijñāna-sahitaṁ
yaj jñātvā mokṣyase'śubhāt // 1

The Blessed Lord said:

I shall now declare to you, who are endowed with reverence, that profoundest of all mystic doctrines and the way to its experience, by which you will be free from the baneful life of Saṁsāra.

Rāja-vidyā rāja-guhyaṁ
pavitraṁ idam uttamam /
pratyakṣ'āvagamaṁ dharmyaṁ
susukhaṁ kartum avyayam // 2

It is a sovereign science, and a profound mystery. Supremely sanctifying, demonstrable by experience, and yielding imperishable results, it is also easy to perform and is in agreement with the moral law.

Aśraddadhānāḥ puruṣā
dharmasy'āsya parantapa /
aprāpya māṁ nivartante
mṛtyu-samsāra-vartmani // 3

Men without faith in this sacred doctrine (who continue to look upon the body as the self) fail to attain Me. They remain caught up in Saṁsāra, the eternally recurring cycle of births and deaths.

Mayā tatam idaṁ sarvaṁ
jagad avyakta-mūrtinā /
mat-sthāni sarva-bhūtāni
na c'āhaṁ teṣv avasthitaḥ // 4

All this world is pervaded by Me, the Unmanifested Being. All objects subsist in Me, but not I in them.

Na ca mat-sthāni bhūtāni
paśya me yogam aiśvaram /
bhūta-bhṛn na ca bhūta-stho
mam'ātmā bhūta-bhāvanaḥ // 5

And yet objects do not abide in Me! Behold My mysterious Divine Power! Source and support of all objects, and yet not abiding in (i.e.not limited by) them!

Yathākāśa-sthito nityaṁ
vāyuḥ sarvatra-go mahān /
tathā sarvāṇi bhūtāni
mat-sthānī'ty upadhāraya // 6

Know that, as the mighty atmosphere ever abides in space, so do all objects abide in Me (without restricting or limiting Me in the least).

Sarva-bhūtāni Kaunteya
prakṛtim yānti māmikām /

kalpa-kṣaye punas tāni
kalp'ādau visṛjāmy aham // 7

At the end of a cosmic cycle, O son of Kunti! all beings resolve into Nature (Prakṛti), which is My own, and at the beginning of a new one (after the period of dissolution or Pralaya is over), I bring them out again.

Prakrtiṁ svām avaṣṭabhya
visṛ jāmi punaḥ-punaḥ /
bhūta-grāmam imaṁ kṛtsnam
avaśaṁ prakṛter vaśāt // 8

Resorting to Prakṛti (Nature) which is My own Power, I send forth again and again this multitude of beings that are without any freedom, owing to Nature's sway over them.

Na ca mām tāni karmāṇi
nibadhnanti dhanañjaya /
udāsīnavad āsīnam
asaktaṁ teṣu karmasu // 9

These activities do not in any way bind me, because I remain detached like one unconcerned in their midst.

Mayā'dhyakṣeṇa prakṛtiḥ
sūyate sacar'ācaram /
hetunā'nena Kaunteya
jagad viparivartate // 10

Under My direction and control, Nature brings out this mighty universe of living and non-living beings. Thus does the wheel of this world revolve.

Avajānanti māṁ mūḍhā
mānuṣīṁ tanum āśritam /
paraṁ bhāvam ajānanto
mama bhūta-mah'eśvaram // 11

Foolish men, without an understanding of My higher nature as the Supreme Lord of all that exists, disregard Me manifested in the human body.

Mogh'āśā mogha-karmāṇo
mogha-jñānā vicetasaḥ /
rākṣasīṁ āsurīṁ c'aiva
prakṛtiṁ mohinīṁ śritāḥ // 12

Futile are the hopes, futile the works, and futile the knowledge of these men of perverted understanding who are deluded by their cruel, proud and passionate nature, characteristic of Rākṣasas and Asuras.

Mah'ātmānas tu māṁ Pārtha
daivīṁ prakṛtim āśritāḥ /
bhajanty ananya-manaso
jñātvā bhūt'ādim avyayam // 13

But the high-souled ones, endowed with virtues characteristic of Devas, understand Me to be the Immutable and the source of all beings, and adore Me with a mind undistracted by anything else.

Satataṁ kīrtayanto māṁ
yatantaś ca dṛḍha-vratāḥ /
namasyantaś ca māṁ bhaktyā
nitya-yuktā upāsate // 14

Strenuous and steadfast in their vows, these ever-integrated devotees worship Me with devotion, always singing My glories and prostrating before Me.

Jñāna-yajñena c'āpy anye
yajanto māṁ upāsate /
ekatvena pṛthaktvena
bahudhā viśvato-mukham // 15

Others, again, who offer wisdom sacrifice to Me, worship Me the

All-inclutive Whole (All-formed)— as the One, as the Distinct, and as the Immanent in all.

Aham kratur ahaṁ yajñaḥ
svadhā'ham aham auṣadham /
mantro'ham aham ev'ājyam
aham agnir aham hutam // 16

I am the sacrifice(*kratu*),I am the worship(*yajña*),I am the ancestral offering (*svadhā*), I am the medicinal herb. Again I am the Vedic hymn, I am the sacrificial ingredients. I am the sacrificial fire, and I am the sacrificial oblation too.

Pitā'ham asya jagato
mātā dhātā pitāmahaḥ /

vedyaṁ pavitram oṁ-kāra
ṛk sāma yajur eva ca //

To this world I am the father, the mother, the grandsire and the sustainer. I am the Holy One to be known, as also the syllable Om, the Ṛk, Sāma and Yajus.

Gatir bhartā prabhuḥ sākṣī
nivāsaḥ śaraṇaṁ suhṛt /
prabhavaḥ pralayaḥ sthānaṁ
nidhānaṁ bījam avyayam // 18

The goal, the support, the Lord, and the consciousness witnessing — all this I am. I am again the abode, the refuge, and the friend of all, as also their origin, their dissolution, their ground, their treasure-house and their seed imperishable.

Tapāmy aham, ahaṁ varṣaṁ
nigṛhṇāmy utsṛjāmi ca /
amṛtaṁ c'aiva mṛtyuś ca
sad asac c'āham Arjuna // 19

I give heat, and I send forth as well as withhold rain. I am, O Arjuna! both immortality and death, both being and non-being.

Traividyā māṁ soma-pāḥ pūta-pāpā
yajñair iṣṭvā svar-gatiṁ prārthayante /

te puṇyam āsādya sur'endra-lokam
aśnanti divyān divi deva-bhogān
// 20

Men versed in the Vedas, cleansed of their sins by the performance of sacrifices attended with the drinking of consecrated Soma juice, pray for heavenly regions (as the reward for adoring Me with those rites). They go to the heaven of Indra, attainable by meritorious deeds, and enjoy heavenly felicities there.

Te tam bhuktva svargā-lokaṁ viśālaṁ
kṣīṇe puṇye martya-lokaṁ viśanti /

evaṁ trayī-dharmam anuprapannā
gatāgataṁ kāma-kāmā
labhante // 21

Having enjoyed the varied felicities of heaven for long, they come back to the world of human beings when their asset of meritorious deeds is exhausted. Thus, being desire-ridden, the followers of the Vedic sacrificial rites stagnate in Saṁsāra, the repetitive state of going and returning.

Ananyāś cintayanto māṁ
ye janāḥ paryupāsate /
teṣāṁ nity'ābhiyuktānāṁ
yoga-kṣemaṁ vahāmy aham // 22

Whoever, being devoted to me solely, engage themselves always in contemplation and worship of Me — to such ever-steadfast devotees I ensure the procurement of all their wants (salvation) and the preservation of their assets (worldly interests).

Ye'py anya-devatā-bhaktā
yajante śraddhayā'nvitāḥ /
te'pi mām eva Kaunteya
yajanty avidhi-pūrvakam // 23

O son of Kuntī! Those devotees who worship even other deities with deep faith, they also are worshipping Me alone, though contrary to injunctions.

Aham hi sarva-yajñānāṁ
bhoktā ca prabhur eva ca /
na tu mām abhijānanti
tattven'ātaś cyavanti te // 24

I am indeed the only enjoyer and the Lord of all sacrifices. But they (the worshippers of other deities) do not understand Me in My true nature (as the object of all worship). So they fall.

Yānti deva-vratā devān
pitṛn yānti pitṛ-vratāḥ /
bhūtāni yānti bhūt'ejyā
yānti mad-yājino'pi mām // 25

The votaries of the deities go to the deities; of the manes, to the manes;

and of the spirits, to the spirits, while My worshippers come to Me.

Patraṁ puṣpaṁ phalaṁ toyaṁ
yo me bhaktyā prayacchati /
tad ahaṁ bhakty-upahṛtam
aśnāmi prayat'ātmanaḥ // 26

Whoever makes an offering to Me with devotion, be it of leaf, flower, fruit or water — that devout offering by a pure-hearted man, I accept with joy.

Yat karoṣi yad aśnāsi
yaj juhoṣi dadāsi yat /
yat tapasyasi Kaunteya
tat kuruṣva mad-arpaṇam // 27

O son of Kuntī! Whatever you do, whatever you eat, whatever you offer in sacrifice, whatever you give as charity, whatever austerity you perform — do that as offering unto Me.

Śubhāśubha-phalair evaṁ
mokṣyase karma-bandhanaih /
sannyāsa-yoga yuktātmā
vimukto mām upaiṣyasi // 28

Thus shall you be freed from the bonds of Karma bearing good and evil fruits. With the heart firmly set on renunciation, you will attain liberation and thereby come to Me.

Samo'ham sarvabhūteṣu
na me dveṣyo'sti na priyaḥ /
ye bhajanti tu māṁ bhaktyā
mayi te teṣu c'āpy aham // 29

I am the same towards all beings. None is hateful, and none dear to Me. But those who worship Me with devotion dwell in Me, and I too dwell in them.

Api cet sudurācāro
bhajate mām ananya-bhāk /
sādhur eva sa mantavyaḥ
samyag vyavasito hi saḥ // 30

Even a confirmed sinner, if he worships Me with unwavering faith and devotion, must verily be considered as righteous; for he has indeed taken the right resolve.

Kṣipraṁ bhavati dharm'ātmā
śaśvac-chāntiṁ nigacchati /
Kaunteya pratijānīhi
na me bhaktaḥ praṇaśyati // 31

Soon will he become righteous and attain to lasting peace. No devotee of Mine will ever perish; you may swear to this effect, O Arjuna!

Mām hi Pārtha vyapāśritya
ye'pi syuḥ pāpa-yonayaḥ /
striyo vaiśyās tathā śudrās
te'pi yānti parāṁ gatim // 32

O son of Pṛithā! Taking refuge in Me, women, Vaiśyas, Śūdras, and likewise even men of inferior birth, attain to the highest spiritual goal.

Kiṁ punar brāhmaṇāḥ puṇyā
bhakta rāja-ṛṣayas tathā /
anityam asukhaṁ lokam
imam prāpya bhajasva mām // 33

Then how much more so in the case of holy Brāhmaṇas and also of devoted royal sages! Having come into this impermanent and unhappy world, engage yourself in My worship.

Man-manā bhava mad-bhakto
madyājī māṁ namas-kuru /

mām ev'aiṣyasi yuktv'aivam
ātmānaṁ mat-parāyaṇaḥ // 34

Let your mind be absorbed in Me. Be devoted to Me, sacrifice unto Me, and bow down to Me. Thus, having Me as your highest goal, and united with Me in mind, you shall come to Me alone.

Chapter X

Divine Glories

Śrī Bhagavān uvāca:

Bhūya eva mahā-bāho
śṛṇu me paramaṁ vacaḥ /
yat te'haṁ prīyamāṇāya
vakṣyāmi hita-kāmyayā // 1

The Blessed Lord said:

Hear again, O mighty armed one, My words on the Supreme Truth. Desirous of your good, I want to declare it to you, who are so beloved of Me.

Na me viduḥ sura-gaṇāḥ
prabhavaṁ na maharṣayaḥ /
aham ādir hi devānāṁ
maharṣīṇāṁ ca sarvaśaḥ // 2

Neither the hosts of gods nor Maharshis (great sages) know my origin, for I am Myself the origin of all those gods and great sages.

Yo māṁ ajam anādiṁ ca
vetti loka-mah'eśvaram /
asaṁmūḍhaḥ sa martyeṣu
sarva-pāpaiḥ pramucyate // 3

He who knows Me as the beginningless, the unborn and the Master of the worlds — he among mortals becomes undeluded, and he is freed from all sins.

Buddhir jñānam asammohaḥ
kṣamā satyam damaḥ śamaḥ /
sukhaṁ duḥkaṁ bhavo'bhāvo
bhayaṁ c'ābhayam eva ca //

Ahiṁsā samatā tuṣṭis
tapo dānaṁ yaśo'yaśaḥ /
bhavanti bhāvā bhūtānāṁ
matta eva pṛthag-vidhāḥ // 4-5

Intelligence, knowledge, sanity, patience, truth, sense-control, mind-control, pleasure, pain, birth, death, fear and also fearlessness; non - injury, same - sightednsss, contentment, austerity, benevolence, fame and obloquy — all these diverse modes of the mind seen in all beings proceed from Me alone, their ultimate sanctioner.

Maharṣayaḥ sapta pūrve
catvāro manavas tathā /
mad-bhāvā mānasā jātā
yeṣāṁ loka imāḥ prajāḥ // 6

The seven great sages (beginning with Marichi) as also the four earlier ones like Sanaka and the rest and the Manus likewise are My emanations, being projections of my thought. All this race of men is their progeny.

Etāṁ vibhūtiṁ yogaṁ ca
mama yo vetti tattvataḥ /
so'vikaṁpena yogena
yujyate n'ātra saṁśayaḥ // 7

He who knows the truth about this manifestation of My Divine majesties and about My power, gets united with Me in steady and unfaltering communion. There is no doubt about this.

Ahaṁ sarvasya prabhavo
mattaḥ sarvaṁ pravartate /
iti matvā bhajante māṁ
budhā bhāva-samanvitāḥ // 8

I am the source of all things, from Me all these go forth — knowing thus the wise ones worship Me, being filled with ecstatic devotional fervour.

Mac-cittā mad-gata-prāṇā
bodhayantaḥ parasparam /
kathayantaś ca māṁ nityaṁ
tuṣyanti ca ramanti ca // 9

With their minds engrossed and their vital energies deeply involved in Me, they are ever contented and delighted by mutually conversing about Me and enlightening each other thereby.

Teṣāṁ satata-yuktānāṁ
bhajatāṁ prīti-pūrvakam /
dadāmi buddhi-yogaṁ taṁ
yena māṁ upayānti te // 10

To those who serve Me with delight and are ever steadfast in spiritual communion, I bestow intuitive understanding by means of which they come to Me.

Teṣām ev'ānukamp'ārtham
aham ajñāna-jaṁ tamaḥ /
nāśayāmy ātma-bhāva-stho
jñāna-dīpena bhāsvatā // 11

Out of sheer compassion for them, residing within as their innermost self, I destroy the darkness born of ignorance in them by the brilliant lamp of wisdom.

Arjuna uvāca:

Paraṁ brahma paraṁ dhāma
pavitraṁ paramaṁ bhavān /
puruṣaṁ śāśvataṁ divyam
ādi-devam ajaṁ vibhum //

Āhus tvām ṛṣayaḥ sarve
deva'rṣir Nāradas tathā /
Asito Devalo Vyāsaḥ
svayaṁ c'aiva bravīṣi me // 12-13

Arjuna said:

Thou art the Supreme Brahman, the Supreme Abode, the Utterly Holy. Thou art the eternal divine Person — the birthless and all-pervading Divinity supreme. All the Rishis proclaim this — the divine sage Nārada as also Asita, Devala and Vyāsa; Thou Thyself too dost tell Me the same.

Sarvam etad ṛtaṁ manye
yan māṁ vadasi Keśava /
na hi te bhagavan vyaktiṁ
vidur devā na dānavāḥ // 14

O Keśava! Whatever Thou hast told me, I deem as true. Verily, O Lord, neither the Devas nor the Dānavas know what Thy manifestations are.

Svyam ev'ātman'ātmānaṁ
vettha tvaṁ Puruṣottama /

bhūta-bhāvana bhūt'eśa
deva-deva jagat-pate // 15

O Thou the highest of all beings! O Creator of all! O Lord of all! O God of gods! O Ruler of the world! Thou art known only to Thyself through self-intuition.

Vaktum arhasy aśeṣeṇa
divyā hy ātma-vibhūtayaḥ /
yābhir vibhūtibhir lokān
imāṁs tvam vyāpya tiṣṭhasi // 16

Deign to speak to me in entirety of those divine manifestations of Thy glory, whereby, pervading all these worlds, Thou abidest in them and beyond.

Katham vidyām aham yogiṁs
tvāṁ sadā paricintayan /
keṣu keṣu ca bhāveṣu
cintyo'si bhagavan mayā // 17

How am I to know Thee, O Yogin, through constant meditation? In what all aspects shouldst Thou be contemplated upon by me, O Lord?

Vistareṇ'ātmano yogaṁ
vibhūtiṁ ca Janārdana /
bhūyaḥ kathaya tṛptir hi
śṛṇvato n'āsti me'mṛtam // 18

O Janārdana! Tell me again and again of Thy divine powers and majesties; for I am ever eager to hear more and more of Thy nectarine words.

Śrī Bhagavān uvāca:

Hanta te kathayisyāmi
divyā hy ātma-vibhūtayaḥ /
prādhānyataḥ Kuru-śreṣṭha
n'āstyanto vistarasya me // 19

The Blessed Lord said:

Behold, O best of the Kurus! I shall declare unto you what My divine self-manifestations are; but I shall mention only the chief of them. For, there is no end to their details.

Aham ātmā Guḍākeśa
sarva-bhūt'āśaya-sthitaḥ /

aham ādiś ca madhyaṁ ca
bhūtānām anta eva ca // 20

O Arjuna! I am the Self residing in the heart of every being. I am their beginning, their life-span, and their end.

Ādityānām ahaṁ Viṣṇur
jyotiṣāṁ ravir aṁśumān /
Marīcir Marutām asmi
nakṣatrāṇām aham śaśī // 21

Of the twelve Ādityas (suns), I am Viṣṇu; among the luminaries I am the radiant sun; among the seven Maruts (winds) I am Marīcī; and of the Nakṣatras (asterisms), I am the moon.

Vedānāṁ sāma-vedo'smi
devānām asmi Vāsavaḥ /
indriyāṇāṁ manaś c'āsmi
bhuatānām asmi cetanā // 22

Of the Vedas, I am the Sāma Veda; among the Devas, I am Indra; of the senses, I am the mind; and in living beings, I am intelligence.

Rudrāṇāṁ Śaṅkaraś c'āsmi
vitt'eśo yakṣa-rakṣasām /
Vasūnāṁ pāvakaś c'āsmi
Meruḥ śikhariṇām aham // 23

Of the eleven Rudras, I am Śaṅkara; among the Demigods and Titans, I am Kubera; of the eight Vasus, I am Agni; among mountains, I am the Meru.

Purodhasāṁ ca mukhyaṁ māṁ
viddhi Pārtha Bṛhaspatiṁ /
senānīnām aham Skandaḥ
sarasāṁ asmi sāgaraḥ // 24

Among the priests, know me to be the chief of them — Bṛhaspati, the priest of the Devas, O Arjuna. Among the war-lords I am Skanda; among the water reservoirs, I am the ocean.

Maha'rṣīṇāṁ Bhṛgur ahaṁ
girām asmy ekam akṣaram /
yajñānāṁ japa-yajño'smi
sthāvarāṇāṁ Himālayaḥ // 25

Among the great sages, I am Bhṛgu; among utterances I am the mono-syllabled 'Om'; among holy offerings, I am the offering of Japa (silent repetition of Divine Names); among immovable objects, I am the mount Himālaya.

Aśvatthaḥ sarva-vṛkṣāṇāṁ
devarṣīṇāṁ ca Nāradaḥ /
gandharvāṇāṁ Citrarathaḥ
siddhānāṁ Kapilo muniḥ // 26

Among all trees, I am the holy fig-tree; among the divine sages, I am Nārada; among celestial artistes, I am Citraratha; among perfected souls, I am Kapila the sage.

Uccaiḥśrvasam aśvānāṁ
viddhi mām amṛt'odbhavam /

Airāvataṁ gaj'endrāṇāṁ
narāṇāṁ ca nar'ādhipam // 27

Among horses know Me to be the nectar-born Uccaiśravas, among the lordly elephants, the white celestial elephant Airāvata; and among men, persons endowed with leadership.

Āyudhānām ahaṁ vajraṁ
dhenūnām asmi kāma-dhuk /
prajanās' c'āsmi Kandarpaḥ
sarpāṇām asmi Vāsukiḥ // 28

Among weapons I am the thunderbolt; among cows, Kāma-dhenu the celestial cow of plenty; among progenitors, Kāma the god of love; and among snakes, Vāsuki.

Anantaś c'āsmi nāgānāṁ
Varuṇo yādasām aham /
pitṛṇām Aryamā c'āsmi
Yamaḥ saṁyamatām aham // 29

Among serpents I am Ananta; among water-dwellers I am Varuṇa; among the manes I am Aryamā; and among the enforcers of law I am Yama.

Prahlādaś c'āsmi daityānāṁ
kālaḥ kalayatām aham /
mṛgāṇāṁ ca mṛg'endro'haṁ
Vainateyaś ca pakṣiṇām // 30

Among Daityas I am Prahlāda; among calculators I am time; among animals I am the lion; and among birds I am Garuḍa.

Pavanaḥ pavatām asmi
Rāmaḥ saśtra-bhṛtām aham /
jhaṣāṇāṁ makaraś c'āsmi
srotasām asmi Jāhnavī // 31

Among purifying agents I am the wind; among warriors I am Rāma; among the fish I am the shark; and among rivers I am the Ganga.

Sargāṇām ādir antaś ca
madhyaṁ c'aiv'āham Arjuna /
adhyātma-vidyā vidyānāṁ
vādaḥ pravadatām aham // 32

O Arjuna! Of the created objects I am the beginning, middle and end; among the sciences, I am the science of the spirit; and in debators I am the power of correct reasoning.

Akṣarāṇām akāro'smi
dvandvaḥ sāmāsikasya ca /
aham ev'ākṣayaḥ kalo
dhātā'haṁ viśvato-mukhaḥ // 33

Among letters I am the letter 'A', among compound word formations I am the copulative (*dvandva*). I am also the never-ending Time and the all-seeing Brahmā (the dispenser of the Karmas of all beings).

Mṛtyuḥ sarva-haraś c'āham
udbhavaś ca bhaviṣyatām /
kīrtiḥ śrīr vāk ca nārīṇāṁ
smṛtir medhā dhṛtiḥ kṣamā // 34

I am the all-destroying Death, and I am the origin of all that are to come too. Among virtues considered as female I am fame, fortune, speech, memory, intelligence, constancy and patience.

Bṛhat-sāma tathā sāmnāṁ
gāyatrī chandasām aham /
māsānāṁ mārgaśīrṣo'haṁ
ṛtūnām kusum'ākaraḥ // 35

Among the Sāma hymns I am the Bṛhatsāman (the Great Chant); among the Vedic metres, I am the Gāyatrī; among months, I am Mārgaśīrṣa (Nov-Dec.) and among seasons, I am the flower-bearing spring.

Dyūtaṁ chalayatām asmi
tejas tejasvinām aham /
jayo'smi vyavasāyo'smi
sattvaṁ sattvavatām aham // 36

I am the dicing of the deceitful, the power of the powerful and the goodness of the good. I am victory, determination and constancy too.

Vṛṣṇīnāṁ Vāsudevo'smi
Pāṇḍavānāṁ Dhanañjayaḥ /
munīnām apy ahaṁ Vyāsaḥ
Kavīnām Uśanā kaviḥ // 37

I am Vāsudeva among the Vṛṣṇis and Arjuna among the Pāṇḍavas. I am Vyāsa among sages, and Śukra among the far-sighted.

Daṇḍo damayatām asmi
nītir asmi jigīṣatām /
maunaṁ c'aiv'āsmi guhyānāṁ
jñānaṁ jñānavatām aham // 38

I am the rod of chastisement in the disciplinarians; I am the wise policy in those seeking success; I am silence in the arts of secrecy; and I am wisdom in the wise.

Yac c'āpi sarva-bhūtānāṁ
bījaṁ tad aham Arjuna /

na tad asti vinā yat syān
māya bhūtaṁ car'ācaram // 39

Of all beings I am the seed, O Arjuna. Whatever exists in this world, living or non-living, none of them can be, if I were not.

Nā'nto'sti mama divyānāṁ
vibhūtīnāṁ paraṁtapa /
eṣa tū'ddeśataḥ prokto
vibhūter vistaro mayā // 40

O great warrior! There is no end to my divine manifestations. What I have expounded forms only a few of them by way of examples.

Yad-yad vibhūtimat sattvaṁ
śrīmad ūrjitam eva va /
tat-tad evā'vagaccha tvaṁ
mama tejo'ṁśa-sambhavam // 41

Whatever there is endowed with extraordinary glory, attractiveness and vigour, know all that to be born of a fragment of My power.

Athavā bahun'aitena
kiṁ jñātena tavā'rjuna /
viṣṭabhy'āham idaṁ kṛtsnaṁ
ek'āṁśena sthito jagat // 42

But then, of what avail is this detailed understanding of my manifestations to you, O Arjuna!

Supporting this mighty universe with but one single fragment of My self, I remain unchanged and transcendent.

Chapter XI

The Cosmic Form

Arjuna uvāca:

Mad-anugrahāya paramaṁ
guhyam adhyātma saṁjñitam /
yat tvay'oktaṁ vacas tena
moho'yaṁ vigato mama // 1

Arjuna said:

Thy instructions on the grand Mystery, the highest spiritual Truth, imparted to me out of Thy abounding grace, have dispelled my delusion.

Bhav'āpyayau hi bhūtānāṁ
śrutau vistaraśo mayā /
tvattaḥ kamala-patr'ākṣa
māhātmyam api c'āvyayam // 2

O lotus-eyed One! From Thee I have heard at length about the origin and dissolution of creatures as also about Thy greatness that knows no decay.

Evam etad yath'āttha tvam
ātmānaṁ param'eśvara /
draṣṭum icchāmi te rūpam
aiśvaraṁ puruṣ'ottama // 3

Thou art, O Lord Supreme, even as what Thou hast declared Thyself to be. (I understand and accept it.) Yet I now desire to see that form of Thine as the Lord of all.

Manyase yadi tac chakyaṁ
mayā draṣṭum iti prabho /
yog'eśvara tato me tvaṁ
darśay'ātmānam avyayam // 4

If, O Lord, Thou thinkest me worthy of experiencing that immutable form of Thine, then deign to reveal the same to me, O Thou Master of all Yoga!

Śrī bhagavān uvāca:

Paśya me Pārtha rūpāṇi
śataśo'tha sahasraśaḥ /

nānā-vidhāni divyāni
nānā-varṇ'ākṛtīni ca // 5

The Blessed Lord said:

Behold, O Partha, My manifold forms in their hundreds and thousands — all divine and all of varied hues and shapes.

Paśy'ādityān Vasūn Rudrān
Aśvinau Marutas tathā /
bahūny adṛṣṭa-pūrvāṇi
paśy'āścaryāṇi Bhārata // 6

Behold the Ādityas and the Vasus, the Rudras and the Aśvins, and the Maruts likewise — behold these marvels unseen by any before, O scion of Bharata's clan!

Ih'aikastham jagat kṛtsnaṁ
paśy'ādya sacar'ācaram /
mama dehe Guḍākeśa
yac c'ānyad draṣṭum icchasi // 7

O conqueror of sleep! Behold here and now the whole of this universe of conscious and unconscious entities as also anything else you desire to experience — all abiding as a unity in My body.

Na tu māṁ śakyase draṣṭum
anen'aiva sva-cakṣuṣā /
divyaṁ dadāmi te cakṣuḥ
paśya me yogaṁ aiśvaram // 8

You cannot have an experience of Me merely with your physical eye. I therefore give you the power of divine vision. Behold with that My power as the Lord of all.

Sañjaya uvāca:

Evam uktvā tato rājan
mahā-yog'eśvaro hariḥ /
darśayāmāsa Pārthāya
paramaṁ rūpam aiśvaram // 9

Sañjaya said:

So saying, Hari, the Master of all spiritual powers, now revealed to Arjuna His transcendent form as the Lord of the universe.

Aneka-vaktra-nayanam
anek'ādbhuta-darśanam /
aneka-divy'ābharaṇaṁ
divy'ānek'odyat'āyudham // 10

Having countless faces and eyes; exhibiting countless features; provoking wonder; bedecked with countless celestial ornaments equipped with countless divine weapons held aloft;

Divya-maly'āmbara-dharaṁ
divya-gandh'ānulepanam /
sarv'āścaryamayaṁ devam
anantaṁ viśvato-mukham // 11

Wearing heavenly garlands and vestments; anointed with celestial unguents and perfumes; replete with incredible, marvellous features — a divinity boundless and all-seeing.

Divi sūrya-sahasrasya
bhaved yugapad utthitā /
yadi bhāḥ sadṛśī sā syād
bhāsas tasya mah'ātmanaḥ // 12

What brilliance there would have been if a thousand suns were to blaze forth all of a sudden in the sky — to that was comparable the splendour of that great Being.

Tatr'aika-sthaṁ jagat kṛtsnaṁ
pravibhaktam anekadhā /

apaśyad deva-devasya
śarīre Pāṇḍavas tadā // 13

There in the body of that God of all divinities, the son of Pāṇḍu then saw the whole universe — a multiplicity abiding unified in His being.

Tataḥ sa vismay'āviṣṭo
hṛṣṭa-romā dhanaṁjayaḥ /
/praṇamya śirasā devaṁ
kṛt'āñjalir abhāṣata // 14

Thereupon Arjuna, struck with amazement and his hairs standing on end, bowed down before the Lord and said with hands folded in salutation.

Arjuna uvāca:

Paśyāmi devāṁs tava deva dehe
sarvāṁs tathā bhūta-viśeṣa-
saṁghān /
brahmāṇam īśaṁ kamal'āsana-
sthaṁ
ṛṣīṁś ca sarvān urgāṁś ca
divyān // 15

Arjuna said:

In Thy form I see, O Lord, all the Devas and all the varied hosts of other beings — the divine Rishis, the celestial serpents and likewise Brahmā the Lord of creation, seated on his lotus throne.

Aneka-bāhū'dara-vaktra-netraṁ
paśyāmi tvām sarvato'nanta-rūpam
n'āntaṁ na madhyaṁ na punas
tav'ādiṁ
paśyāmi viśveśvara viśva-rūpa // 16

I see Thee in Thy all encompassing form everywhere — with myriad arms, myriad trunks, myriad mouths, myriad eyes. O Lord of all! O the All-formed! I see not Thy beginning, Thy middle, or Thy end.

Kirīṭinaṁ gadinaṁ cakriṇaṁ ca

tejo-rāśiṁ sarvato dīptimantam /

paśyāmi tvāṁ durnirīkṣyaṁ
samantād
dīpt'ānalārka-dyutim
aprameyam // 17

I see Thee, boundless Being, diademed and armed with mace and discus, shining everywhere as a mass of light, and difficult to look at, like the blazing fire or the incandescent sun.

Tvam akṣaraṁ paramaṁ vedita-
vyaṁ
tvam asya viśvasya paraṁ
nidhānam /
tvam avyayaḥ śāśvata-dharma- goptā
sanātanas tvaṁ puruṣo
mato me // 18

In my view Thou art the Supreme Imperishable Being to be realised — the world's ultimate refuge and the guardian of eternal law, most ancient and perennial.

Anādi-madhy'āntam ananta-vīryam
ananta-bāhuṁ śaśi-sūrya-netram /
paśyāmitvāṁ dīpta-hutāśa-vaktraṁ
sva-tejasā viśvam idaṁ
tapantam // 19

I see Thee — beginningless, middleless and endless; infinite in puissance; of boundless energy active everywhere; having the sun and the moon for eyes; with a face luminous like a flaming fire; and with spiritual radiance energising everything.

Dyāvā-pṛthivyor idam antaraṁ hi
vyāptaṁ tvay'aikena diśaś ca sarvāḥ
dṛṣṭvā'dbhutaṁ rūpam ugraṁ tav' edaṁ
loka-trayaṁ pravyathitaṁ mah'ātman // 20

O High-souled One! All the three worlds tremble with fear at the sight of this wondrous, awe-inspiring form of Thine — the one existence that fills all space betwixt heaven and earth and all the quarters as well.

Amī hi tvāṁ sura-saṅghā viśanti
kecid bhītāḥ prāñjalayo gṛṇanti /

svastī'ty uktvā maha'rṣi-siddha-
saṅghāḥ
stuvanti tvāṁ stutibhiḥ
puṣkalābhiḥ // 21

Verily, these bands of Devas enter into Thee, while others, awe-struck, stand with hands joined in salutation. Hosts of sages and celestial singers cry 'Hail' unto Thee, and extol Thee with hymns of abounding praise.

Rudrādityā Vasavo ye ca Sādhyā
Viśve'śvinau Marutaś c'oṣmapās ca
Gandharva-yakṣ'āsura-siddha-
saṁghā
vīkṣante tvāṁ vismitāś c'aiva
sarve // 22

And the Rudras, Ādityas, Vasus and Sādhyas; Viśvas, Aśvins, Maruts and Manes; and the hosts of Gandharvas, Yakṣas, Asuras and Siddhas — all view Thee in utter amazement.

Rūpaṁ mahat te bahu-vaktra-
netraṁ
mahā-bāho bahu-bāh'ūru-pādam /
bah'ūdaraṁ bahu-daṁṣṭrā-karālaṁ
dṛṣṭvā lokāḥ pravyathitās
tathā' ham // 23

At the sight of Thy stupendous form, with faces, eyes, arms, trunks, thighs and legs in myriads, and Thy numerous fangs of forbidding appearance — the whole world, O mighty one, is trembling in awe, even as I.

Nabhaḥ-spṛśaṁ dīptam aneka-varṇaṁ
vyātt'ānanaṁ dīpta-viśāla-netram /
dṛṣṭvā hi tvāṁ pravyathit'āntarātmā
dhṛtiṁ na vindāmi śamaṁ ca Viṣṇo // 24

When I see Thy form reaching up to the skies and shining in varied hues, when I see Thy face with mouth wide open and eyes large and glowing bright, I feel shaken to the core of my being with awe. O All-pervading One! My strength is exhausted and my mind is without peace.

Daṁṣṭrā-karālani ca te mukhāni
dṛṣṭv'aiva kāl'ānala-sannibhāni /
diśo na jāne na labhe ca śarma
prasīda dev'eśa jagan-nivāsa // 25

Even by beholding Thy faces, resembling the fire of cosmic destruction and striking terror with their fangs, I lose all sense of direction as also my presence of mind. O Thou the Lord of all and the home of the worlds! Be propitious unto me!

Amī ca tvāṁ Dhṛtarāṣṭrasya putrāḥ
sarve sah'ai'vā'vani-pāla-saṅghaiḥ
Bhīṣmo Droṇaḥ sūta-putras tathā' sau
sahā'smadīyair api yodha-
mukhyaiḥ //

Vaktrāṇi te tvaramāṇā viśanti
daṁṣṭrā-karālāni bhay'ānakāni /
kecid vilagnā dasan'āntareṣu
saṁdṛśyante cūrṇitair
uttamāṅgaiḥ // 26-27

All these hosts of kings, along with the sons of Dhṛtarāṣṭra, Bhīṣma, Droṇa and yonder Karṇa, as also the principal warriors on our side — all are rushing headlong into Thy fearful mouth set with terrible fangs. Some are seen with their heads crushed and caught in the gaps of Thy teeth.

Yathā nadīnāṁ bahavo'mbu-vegāḥ
samudram ev'ābhimukhā dravanti /

tathā tav'āmī nara-loka-vīrā
viśanti vaktrāṇy abhivijvalanti // 28

As the swift-flowing waters of numerous rivers rush verily towards the sea, so these heroes among men are rushing into Thy flaming mouth.

Yathā pradīptam jvalanaṁ pataṅgā
viśanti nāśāya samṛddha-vegāḥ /
tath'aiva nāśāya viśanti lokās
tav'āpi vaktrāṇi
samṛddha-vegāḥ // 29

As moths swarm swiftly into a flaming fire and perish, so do these men rush headlong into Thy mouth to meet with sure destruction.

Lelihyase grasamānaḥ samantāt
lokān samagrān vadanair jvaladbhiḥ /
tejobhir āpūrya jagat samagraṁ
bhāsas tav'ogrāḥ pratapanti
Viṣṇo // 30

Thou lappest up all these worlds around, devouring them with Thy flaming mouth. Thy lustre, striking awe into the minds of all, fills this entire universe with its radiance and scorches it, O Viṣṇu!

Ākhyāhi me ko bhavān ugra-rūpo
namo'stu te Deva-vara prasīda /
vijñātum icchāmi bhavantam ādyaṁ
na hi prajānāmi tava pravṛttim // 31

Deign to tell me who Thou art with this awe-inspiring form. To Thee, O Supreme Lord, my salutation, and also my prayers for Thy grace. I wish to know more about Thee, the Primal Being, as also of Thy purpose here, of which I am in ignorance.

Śrī Bhagavān uvāca:
Kālo'smi loka-kṣaya-kṛt pravṛddho
lokān samāhartum iha pravṛttaḥ /
ṛte'pi tvāṁ na bhaviṣyanti sarve
ye'vasthitāḥ pratyanīkeṣu yodhāḥ // 32

The Blessed Lord said:

I am the mighty world destroying Time, engaged here in annihilating all beings. Even without you, not one of all the warriors arrayed in these rival armies shall survive.

Tasmāt tvam uttiṣṭha yaśo labhasva
jitvā śatrūn bhuṅkṣva rājyaṁ
samṛddham /
may'aiv'aite nihatāḥ pūrvam eva
nimitta-mātraṁ bhava
savyasācin // 33

Therefore arise! Win renown! And destroying your enemies, enjoy the prosperous kingdom. For, these warriors have already been slain by Me. Be you but an instrument thereof, O thou master-bowman, Arjuna.

Dronaṁ ca bhīṣmaṁ ca
Jayadrathaṁ ca
Karṇam tathā'nyān api yodha-vīrān /
mayā hatāṁs tvaṁ jahi mā
vyathiṣṭhā
yudhyasva jetāsi raṇe sapatnān // 34

Kill Droṇa and Bhīṣma, Jayadratha and Karṇa, as also these other heroic warriors, who are already doomed by Me. Fight on, and you shall conquer the enemies in battle.

Sañjaya uvāca:

Etac chrutvā vacanaṁ Keśavasya
kṛtāñjalir vepamānaḥ Kirīṭī /

namas-kṛtvā bhūya ev'āha Kṛṣṇaṁ
sagadgadaṁ bhīta-bhītaḥ
praṇamya //35

Sañjaya said:

Hearing this declaration of Kṛṣṇa, Arjuna, with his frame trembling, saluted Him again and again with joined palms. Prostrating himself before Him in utter awe, Arjuna addressed Him in faltering voice.

Arjuna uvāca:

Sthāne Hṛṣīkeśa tava prakīrtyā
jagat prahṛṣyaty anurajyate ca /

rakṣāṁsi bhītāni diśo dravanti
sarve namsyanti ca
siddha-saṅghāḥ // 36

Arjuna said:

Rightly do the worlds rejoice and delight in glorifying Thee. In Thy presence the Rākṣasas melt away in fear in all directions, while the hosts of Siddhas bow in adoration.

Kasmāc ca te na nameran mahātman
garīyase brahmaṇo'py ādi-kartre /
ananta dev'eśa jagan-nivāsa
tvam akṣaraṁ sad asat
tat-paraṁ yat // 37

O High-souled one! Why should they not bow down to Thee who art the highest of all beings and the primal cause of even Brahmā the creator! O Infinite One! O Lord of all Gods and the Abode of all the worlds! Thou art that Imperishable Being who is both existence (effect condition) and non-existence (causal state) as also that which is beyond them both.

Tvaṃ ādi-devaḥ puruṣaḥ purāṇas /
tvam asya viśvasya paraṁ nidhānam /
vettā'si vedyaṁ ca paraṁ ca dhāma /
tvayā tataṁ viśvam anantarūpa // 38

Thou art the first of all divinities and the most ancient of all beings. Thou art the ultimate haven of rest and safety for the worlds. Thou art both the knower and the known as also the supreme Abode. O Thou of countless forms! By Thee the whole universe is pervaded.

Vāyur Yamo'gnir Varuṇaḥ śaśāṅkaḥ
Prajāpatis tvaṁ prapitāmahaś ca /
namo namas te'stu sahasra-kṛtvaḥ
punaś ca bhūyo'pi namo
namas te // 39

Manifested as Vāyu the god of winds, as Yama the god of death, as Varuṇa the god of the seas, and as the moon with the hare-mark on the face — Thou art the Progenitor of all and the source of him as well. Hail, hail unto Thee a thousand times! Hail, and hail again and yet again.

Namaḥ purastād atha pṛṣṭhatas te
namo'stu te sarvata eva sarva /
ananta-vīry'āmita-vikramas tvaṁ
sarvaṁ samāpnoṣi tato'si
sarvaḥ // 40

Salutations unto Thee, the All-formed, from before, from behind and from all directions! Infinite in puissance and limitless in might, Thou pervadest everything and Thou art verily the All.

Sakh'eti matvā prasabhaṁ yad uktaṁ
he Kṛṣṇa he Yādava he sakh'eti /
ajānatā mahimānaṁ tav'edaṁ
mayā pramādāt praṇayena vāpi //

Yac c'āvahās'ārtham asatkṛto'si
vihāra-śayy'āsana-bhojaneṣu /
eko'thavā'py acyuta tat-samakṣaṁ
tat kṣāmaye tvām aham
aprameyam //41-42

O undecaying One! If, without knowing Thy greatness and taking Thee only to be a friend, I have, out of ignorance or love, alone or even in company, addressed Thee discourteously in fun, while playing relaxing, sitting or feasting, with words such as, "O Kṛṣṇa! O Yādava!" — I beseech Thee, O Boundless One, do pardon me for the same!

Pitā'si lokasya car'ācarasya
tvam asya pūjyaś ca gurur garīyān /
na tvat-samo'sty abhyadhikaḥ kuto'nyo
loka-traye'py apratima prabhāva //43

Thou art the father of the world — of all that is moving and unmoving. Thou art the object of its worship, the most venerable of its Teachers. In all the worlds there is not another equal to Thee, much less one greater, O Thou of incomparable puissance!

Tasmāt praṇamya praṇidhāya kāyaṁ
prasādaye tvām aham īśam īḍyam /
pit'eva putrasya sakh'eva sakhyuḥ
priyaḥ priyāy'ārhasi deva sodhum // 44

Therefore greeting Thee with my body stretched in prostration, I beseech Thee, O worshipful Lord, to be gracious unto me. Bear with me as a father with a son, as a friend with a friend, and as a lover with his beloved.

Adṛṣṭa-pūrvaṁ hṛṣito'smi dṛṣṭvā
bhayena ca pravyathitaṁ mano me /
tad eva me darśaya deva rūpaṁ
prasīda dev'eśa jagan-nivāsa // 45

Seeing this form unseen before, I am overjoyed but my mind is also perturbed with fear. Reveal to me that other familiar form of Thine and be gracious unto me, O Thou God of all gods, and Indwelling Spirit of the worlds.

Kirītinaṁ gadinaṁ cakra-hastam
icchāmi tvāṁ draṣṭum ahaṁ
tath'aiva /
ten'aiva rūpeṇa catur-bhujena
sahasra-bāho bhava
viśva-mūrte //46

I desire to see Thee as before crowned with a diadem, and holding a mace and discus in hand. Deign to assume that four-armed shape, O Thou of a thousand arms and of universal form!

Śrī Bhagavān uvāca:
Mayā prasannena tav'ārjun'edaṁ
rūpaṁ paraṁ darśitam ātmayogāt /
tejomayaṁ viśvam anantam ādyaṁ
yan me tvad-anyena na
dṛṣṭapūrvam // 47

The Blessed Lord said:

Out of My grace, I have, by My divine power, revealed to you this transcendent form of Mine — infinite, primeval, radiant and all-inclusive. Never has it been seen by any one before except by you.

Na veda-yajñ'ādhyayanair na dānair
na ca kriyābhir na tapobhir ugraiḥ /
evaṁ-rūpaḥ śakya ahaṁ nṛ-loke
draṣṭuṁ tvad-anyena
Kurupravīra //48

Except by you (on whom My grace has been bestowed), none in this world of men could see Me in this Cosmic Form — be it by Vedic study, by sacrifice, by good works, by rituals, or by severe austerities.

Mā te vyathā mā ca vimūḍhabhāvo
dṛṣṭvā rūpaṁ ghoram īdṛṅ
mam'edam

vyapeta-bhīḥ prīta-manāḥ punas tvaṁ
tad eva me rūpam idaṁ
prapaśya // 49

Fear not; nor be bewildered at seeing this awe-inspiring form of Mine. With fear assuaged and a heart full of joy, behold now this, My familiar form, again!

Sañjaya uvāca:

Ity Arjunaṁ Vāsudevas tath'oktvā
svakaṁ rūpaṁ darśayāmāsa bhūyaḥ /
āśvāsayāmāsa ca bhītam enaṁ
bhūtvā punaḥ saumya-vapur
mah'ātmā //50

Sañjaya said:

Saying thus to Arjuna, Krishna revealed again his own familiar form. Having thus assumed that gentle form, the Exalted One comforted the awe-struck Arjuna over again.

Arjuna uvāca:

Dṛṣṭv'edam mānuṣaṁ rūpaṁ
tava saumyaṁ Janārdana /
idānīm asmi saṁvṛttaḥ
sacetāḥ prakṛtiṁ gataḥ // 51

Arjuna said:

Seeing this gentle human form of Thine, O Janārdana, I am now composed and restored to my natural state of mind.

Śrī Bhagavān uvāca:

Sudurdarśam idaṁ rūpaṁ
dṛṣṭavān asi yan mama /
devā apy asya rūpasya
nityaṁ darśana-kāṅkṣiṇaḥ // 52

The Blessed Lord said:

This form of Mine which you have seen is extremely difficult to behold. Even Devas themselves are ever eager to see it.

N'āhaṁ vedair na tapasā
na dānena na c'ejyayā /

śakya evaṁ-vidho draṣṭuṁ
dṛṣṭavān asi māṁ yathā // 53

Neither by Vedic study, nor by austerities, nor by charities, nor by sacrifices could one behold Me in the way you have done.

Bhaktyā tv'ananyayā śakya
aham evaṁ-vidho'rjuna /
jñātuṁ draṣṭuṁ ca tattvena
praveṣṭuṁ ca paraṁtapa // 54

But, O Arjuna, thou great warrior! Through unswerving devotion this form of Mine may be known in truth and in reality, may be experienced and entered into.

Mat-karma-kṛn mat-paramo
mad-bhaktaḥ saṅga-varjitaḥ /
nirvairaḥ sarva-bhūteṣu
yaḥ sa mām eti Pāṇḍava // 55

Whoever works for Me, looking upon Me as the goal; whoever is My devotee, free from attachments and from antagonism to any being — such a man, O son of Pāṇḍu, shall enter into Me.

Chapter XII

Loving Devotion

Arjuna uvāca:

Evaṁ satata-yuktā ye
bhaktās tvāṁ paryupāsate /
ye c'āpy akṣaram avyaktaṁ
teṣāṁ ke yoga-vittamāḥ // 1

Arjuna said:

There are Thy ever-steadfast devotees who love and worship Thee in the above way (as the Divine Person); there are again others who contemplate on Thee as the

Imperishable Unmanifest (Impersonal Absolute) — which of these has a greater understanding of Yoga.

Śrī Bhagavān uvāca:

Mayy āveśya mano ye māṁ
nitya-yuktā upāsate /
śraddhayā paray'opetās
te me yukta-tamā matāḥ // 2

The Blessed Lord said:

Those I consider as the most perfect in Yoga, who, with their minds fixed intently on Me in steadfast love, worship Me with absolute faith.

Ye tv akṣaram anirdeśyam
avyaktaṁ paryupāsate /

sarvatra-gam acintyaṁ ca
kūṭa-stham acalaṁ dhruvam //

Saṁniyamy'endriya-grāmaṁ
sarvatra sama-buddhayaḥ
te prāpnuvanti mām eva
sarva-bhūta-hite ratāḥ // 3-4

Those who are devoted to the Imperishable (the Impersonal Absolute) — who is the firm support of the world and is also undefinable, unmanifested, transcendent, motionless, eternal and all-pervading, — even they reach Me alone, striving with their senses controlled, and with mind tranquillised and set on the welfare of all.

Kleśo'dhikataras teṣāṁ
avyakt'āsakta-cetasām
avyaktā hi gatir duḥkhaṁ
dehavadbhir avāpyate // 5

The obstacles facing those devoted to the Impersonal Absolute are far greater; for the way of any unclear ideal is difficult for an embodied being (the body-centred man) to understand or follow.

Ye tu sarvāṇi karmāṇi
mayi saṁnyasya mat-parāḥ /
ananyen'aiva yogena
māṁ dhyāyanta upāsate //

Teṣāṁ ahaṁ samuddhartā
mṛtyu-saṁsāra-sāgarāt /

bhavāmi nacirāt Pārtha
mayy āveśita-cetasām // 6-7

But, O son of Pṛthā, soon will I lift from this ocean of death-bound worldly existence, those whose minds are ever set on Me — those who abandon to Me the fruits of all their actions together with the sense of agency thereof, and who worship Me, meditating on Me as their sole refuge and their only love.

Mayy eva mana ādhatsva
mayi buddhiṁ niveśaya /
nivasiṣyasi mayy eva
ata ūrdhvaṁ na saṁśayaḥ // 8

Fix your mind on Me alone; let your reason penetrate into Me; without doubt you will then abide in Me alone for ever more.

Atha cittaṁ samādhātuṁ
na śaknoṣi mayi sthiram /
abhyāsa-yogena tato
māṁ icch'āptum Dhanañjaya // 9

If you are unable to fix your mind steadily on Me (even at the start), then try to reach Me through the systematic practice of concentration.

Abhyāse'py asamartho'si
mat-karma-paramo bhava /
mad-artham api karmāṇi
kurvan siddhim avāpsyasi // 10

If you are not capable of practising systematic concentration, then devote yourself whole heartedly to works of service to Me (consisting in external worship and discharge of duties for My sake). Thus working for Me, man can attain to perfection.

Ath'aitad apy aśakto'si
kartuṁ mad-yogam āśritaḥ /
sarva-karma-phala-tyāgaṁ
tataḥ kuru yat'ātmavān // 11

If even this is too difficult for you to perform, then taking refuge in Me, and thus controlling the mind, give up the fruits of all your actions (recognising Me as their agent and enjoyer).

Śreyo hi jñānam abhyāsāt
jñānād dhyānaṁ viśiṣyate /
dhyānāt karma-phala-tyāgas
tyāgāc chāntir anantaram // 12

Than (a mere formal) practice of disciplines, a clear intellectual understanding (of the doctrine) is better. Than such understanding, meditation is better. Even better than meditation is the abandonment of the fruits of action. For, such abandonment (of the fruits of works and sense of their agency) is immediately followed by peace.

Adveṣṭā sarva-bhūtānāṁ
maitraḥ karuṇa eva ca /
nirmamo nirahaṁkāraḥ
sama-duḥkha-sukhaḥ kṣamī //

santuṣṭaḥ satataṁ yogī
yat'ātmā dṛḍha-niścayaḥ /
mayy arpita-mano-buddhir
yo mad-bhaktaḥ sa
me priyaḥ // 13-14

Friendly and compassionate to all and without any touch of hatred; devoid of possessiveness and arrogance; ever content and contemplative; alike in happiness and misery; self-controlled and firm in conviction; dedicated to Me with all his heart and all his soul — dear to Me is a man who is thus devoted.

Yasmān n'odvijate loko
lokān n'odvijate ca yaḥ /
harṣ'āmarṣa-bhay'odvegair
mukto yaḥ sa ca me priyaḥ // 15

Who causes fear to none and whom none can frighten, who is thus free from the agitation of the moods caused by euphoria, anger, and excitement — such a person too is dear to Me.

Anapekṣaḥ śucir dakṣa
udāsīno gata-vyathaḥ /

sarvārambha-parityāgī
yo mad-bhaktaḥ sa me priyaḥ // 16

Desireless, pure, resourceful, unattached, unworried and without any sense of self-centred agency — a devotee thus endowed is dear to Me.

Yo na hṛṣyati na dveṣṭi
na śocati na kāṅkṣati /
śubh'āśubha-parityāgī
bhaktimān yaḥ sa me priyaḥ // 17

He who is free from elation, anger, sorrow, and craving, who neither seeks the pleasant nor shuns the unpleasant — dear to Me is the man who is thus devoted.

Samaḥ śatrau ca mitre ca
tathā mān'āpamānayoḥ /
śītoṣṇa-sukha-duḥkheṣu
samaḥ saṅga-vivarjitaḥ //

Tulya-nindā-stutir maunī
saṁtuṣṭo yena kenacit /
aniketaḥ sthira-matir
bhaktimān me priyo naraḥ // 18-19

Alike to friend and foe, alike in honour and insult, alike in heat and cold, alike in praise and blame — unattached, contented, homeless, and steady in mind — dear to Me is a man who is thus devoted.

Ye tu dharmy'āmṛtam idaṁ
yath'oktaṁ paryupāsate /

śraddadhānā mat-paramā
bhaktās te'tīva me priyāḥ // 20

Whosoever even seeks to follow the virtuous path to Immortality thus set forth, with a mind full of faith and acceptance of Me as their supreme goal — exceedingly dear to Me are men who are thus devoted.

Chapter XIII

The Knower and The Known

Śrī Bhagavān uvāca:

Idaṁ śarīraṁ Kaunteya
kṣetram ity abhidhīyate /
etad yo vetti taṁ prāhuḥ
kṣetra-jña iti tad-vidaḥ // 1

The Blessed Lord said:

This body, O son of Kunti, is called the Kṣetra, the field (because the fruits of action are reaped in it). He who knows it (as his property) is the Kṣetrajña or the Spirit who knows the field. So say those versed in this subject.

Kṣetra-jñaṁ c'āpi māṁ viddhi
sarva-kṣetreṣu Bhārata /
kṣetra-kṣetra-jñayor jñānaṁ
yat taj jñānaṁ mataṁ mama // 2

Know Me, O scion of the Bharata race, to be the Kṣetrajña (the Spirit) in all Kṣetras (bodies). The knowledge of the distinction between Kṣetra and Kṣetrajña alone is real knowledge according to Me.

Tat kṣetraṁ yac ca yādṛk ca
yad-vikāri yataś ca yat /
sa ca yo yat-prabhāvaś ca
tat samāsena me śṛṇu // 3

Hear from Me in brief what the Kṣetra is, of what nature it is, what its modifications are, and from what causes what effects have sprung. Also know who the Kṣetrajña is and what his powers are.

Ṛṣibhir bahudhā gītaṁ
chandobhir vividhaiḥ pṛthak /
brahma-sūtra-padaiś c'aiva
hetumadbhir viniścitaiḥ // 4

In many and different ways have the Ṛṣis sung about this subject in metres of varying description. The well-reasoned and definitive aphorisms of the Brahma-sūtras too have discussed it.

Mahā-bhūtāny ahaṁkāro
buddhir avyaktam eva ca /
indriyāṇi daś'aikaṁ ca
pañca c'endriya-gocarāḥ //

Icchā dveṣaḥ sukhaṁ duḥkhaṁ
saṁghātaś cetanā dhṛtiḥ
etat kṣetraṁ samāsena
savikāram udāhṛtam // 5-6

The five great elements, the I-sense, the intellect, and the Unmanifested (Root Matter); the ten organs along with the mind as the eleventh, and the five objects of the senses; desire, hatred, pleasure and pain; the body, consciousness, and will — such is a brief description of the Kṣetra with all its modifications.

Amānitvam adambhitvam
ahiṁsā kṣāntir ārjavam /
ācāry'opāsanaṁ śaucaṁ
sthairyam ātma-vinigrahaḥ // 7

Freedom from self-importance, unpretentiousness, non - violence, patience, straight - forwardness, service of the teacher, cleanliness, steadfastness, and self-control;

Indriy'ārtheṣu vairāgyam
anahaṁkāra eva ca /
janma-mṛtyu-jarā-vyādhi-
duḥka-doṣ'ānudarśanam // 8

Abhorrence of sensuality, self-effacement and perception of evil and misery in birth, death, old age and sickness;

Asaktir anabhiṣvaṅgaḥ
putra-dāra-gṛhādiṣu /
nityaṁ ca sama-cittatvam
iṣṭ'āniṣṭ'opapattiṣu // 9

Detachment from property and family members, non-identification with them and their fortunes, and constant evenness of mind in favourable and unfavourable situations;

Mayi c'ānanya-yogena
bhaktir avyabhicāriṇī /

vivikta-deśa-sevitvam
aratir jana-saṁsadi // 10

Practice of unswerving devotion through contemplation on Me as one's 'own' (or on Me in non-separation), resort to solitude and abhorrence of vulgar company;

Adhyātma-jñāna-nityatvaṁ
tattva-jñān'ārtha-darśanam /
etat jñānam iti proktam
ajñānaṁ yad ato'nyathā // 11

Constant application to the study of spiritual texts and practice of spiritual disciplines, and a clear comprehension of the goal of spiritual enlightenment and the destiny of man

— all these described before constitute knowledge; what all is opposed to it is ignorance.

Jñeyaṁ yat tat pravakṣyāmi
yat jñātv'āmṛtam aśnute /
anādimat paraṁ brahma
na sat tan n'āsad ucyate // 12

I shall now declare the Object which ought to be known, by knowing which one attains to immortality. It is the Supreme Brahman, the eternal Being who cannot be described either as existent or non-existent (in the way sense-bound material objects are described).

Sarvataḥ pāṇi-pādaṁ tat
sarvato'kṣi-śiro-mukham /
sarvataḥ śrutimal loke
sarvam āvṛtya tiṣṭhati // 13

His hands and feet are everywhere. His eyes, ears and mouth grasp everything. His face is in all directions. He is the transcendent Spirit, enveloping all that exists.

Sarv'endriya-guṇ'ābhāsaṁ
sarv'endriya-vivarjitam /
asaktaṁ sarva-bhṛc c'aiva
nirguṇaṁ guṇa-bhoktṛ ca // 14

By His power the faculties of the senses function, but sense organs He has none. He is the support of all things, but they do not affect Him. He transcends Nature and its functions, but these constitute the objects for His enjoyment.

Bahir antaś ca bhūtānām
acaraṁ caram eva ca /
sūkṣmatvāt tad avijñeyaṁ
dūrasthaṁ c'āntike ca tat // 15

He is within and without all beings. Though unmoving, He looks like one moving (because He is everywhere). He is both far and near — far to the ignorant, and near to the knowing ones. Owing to subtlety, He cannot be known like gross objects.

Avibhaktaṁ ca bhūteṣu
vibhaktam iva ca sthitam /
bhūta-bhartṛ ca tat jñeyaṁ
grasiṣṇu prabhaviṣṇu ca // 16

He, (the Brahman) whom aspirants seek to know, is the impartible Whole, yet does He seem to dwell in all beings as if divided into many. He is the generator and supporter of all beings, and their devourer too.

Jyotiṣām api taj jyotis
tamasaḥ param ucyate /
jñānaṁ jñeyaṁ jñāna-gamyaṁ
hṛdi sarvasya dhiṣṭhitam // 17

The self-luminous light of consciousness revealing even all that is luminous, He is beyond obscuration by the darkness of ignorance. He, the light of knowledge, He, the quest of knowledge, He, the way to whom is knowledge — in the innermost recess of all beings is He established.

Iti kṣetraṁ tathā jñānaṁ
jñeyaṁ c'oktaṁ samāsataḥ /
mad-bhakta etad vijñāya
mad-bhāvāy'opapadyate // 18

Thus has been briefly expounded what the Kṣetra (material Nature) is, as also what constitutes knowledge and the object of knowledge. My devotee who understands these verities becomes worthy of My state.

Prakṛtiṁ puruṣaṁ c'aiva
viddhy anādī ubhāvapi /
vikārāṁś ca guṇāṁś c'aiva
viddhi prakṛti-saṁbhavān // 19

Know both Prakṛti (Nature) and Puruṣa (Spirit) to be beginningless, eternal verities. Know also that all changeful objects and attributes (that constitute the world of daily experience) are sprung from Prakṛti.

Kārya-kāraṇa-kartṛtve
hetuḥ prakṛtir ucyate /
puruṣaḥ sukha-duḥkhānāṁ
bhoktṛtve hetur ucyate // 20

Prakṛti is the cause of the formation and functioning of the body and the senses, while it is the Puruṣa that experiences pleasure and pain, joy and sorrow.

Puruṣaḥ prakṛti-stho hi
bhuṅkte prakṛti-jān guṇān /
kāraṇaṁ guṇa-saṅgo'sya
sad-asad-yoni-janmasu // 21

Seated in bodies, which are the products of Prakṛti, the Puruṣa enjoys the objects and qualities born of Prakṛti. Attachment to these objects is the cause of the Spirit getting embodiments in evil or exalted wombs.

Upadraṣṭā'numantā ca
bhartā bhoktā mah'eśvaraḥ /

param'ātm'eti c'āpy ukto
dehe'smin puruṣaḥ paraḥ // 22

In this body there is also the Transcendent and the Supreme Spirit, who is described as the Supreme Self and Sovereign Lord, the unconcerned Witness, the Sanctioner, the Supporter and the Enjoyer.

Ya evam vetti puruṣaṁ
prakṛtiṁ ca guṇaiḥ saha /
sarvathā vartamāno'pi
na sa bhūyo'bhijāyate // 23

Whoever thus knows the Puruṣa (Spirit) and Prakṛti (Nature) along with its effects, will never be born again, whatever be his mode of living.

Dhyānen'ātmani paśyanti
kecid ātmānam ātmanā /
anye sāṁkhyena yogena
karma-yogena c'āpare // 24

There are some who perceive the Ātman within themselves by the practice of meditation with a purified mind. There are also others who approach Him through the discipline of knowledge or of work.

Anye tvevam ajānantaḥ
śrutvā'nyebhya upāsate /
te'pi c'ātitaranty eva
mṛtyuṁ śruti-parāyaṇāḥ // 25

There are still others, who, being unfit to follow the disciplines described before — for they lack the knowledge of the Yoga Sāstra and the Vedas —, adopt forms of worship (devotional disciplines) under instruction from teachers or elders. Full of faith in these instructions heard, and following them sincerely as their only refuge, they too certainly overcome the cycle of births and deaths.

Yāvat saṁjāyate kiñcit
sattvaṁ sthāvara-jaṅgamaṁ /
kṣetra-kṣetrajña-saṁyogāt
tad viddhi Bharata'rṣabha // 26

O thou the best of the Bharata clan! Whatever there is born — whether moving or unmoving — it has come into being due to the union of Kṣetra (body) and Kṣetrajña (Spirit).

Samaṁ sarveṣu bhūteṣu
tiṣṭhantaṁ param'eśvaram /
vinaśyatsv avinaśyantaṁ
yaḥ paśyati sa paśyati // 27

He really sees who perceives the Supreme Lord alike in everything — as the Imperishable Substance abiding amidst perishing phenomena.

Samaṁ paśyan hi sarvatra
samavasthitam īśvaram /
na hinasty ātmanā'tmānaṁ
tato yāti parāṁ gatim // 28

For, he who perceives the Lord's presence alike everywhere no longer works against his own spiritual well-being (by mistaking the ego for the true spiritual Self as men in ignorance do). He therefore attains to the Supreme Goal.

Prakṛty'aiva ca karmāṇi
kriyamāṇāni sarvaśaḥ /
yaḥ paśyati tathā'tmānam
akartāraṁ sa paśyati // 29

He is the real seer who perceives that Prakṛti (i.e., one's body-mind born of Prakṛti) alone is doing all works and that the Ātman, the true spiritual self, is the actionless witness.

Yadā bhūta-pṛthag-bhāvam
eka-stham anupaśyati /
tata eva ca vistāraṁ
brahma saṁpadyate tadā // 30

When one perceives the manifold objects as centred in the One and as evolved from It as well — then he attains Brahman.

Anāditvān nirguṇatvāt
paramātmā'yam avyayaḥ /
śarīra-stho'pi Kaunteya
na karoti na lipyate // 31

That highest Self, being the immutable and unoriginated Spirit beyond Nature, is free from all action and stain, though dwelling in the body.

Yathā sarva-gataṁ saukṣmyād
ākāśaṁ n'opalipyate /
sarvatr'āvasthito dehe
tathā'tmā n'opalipyate // 32

Just as the all-pervading Ākāśa, because of its subtlety, is not stained by anything, so this Ātman, though abiding in all bodies, is never affected by any impurity.

Yathā prakāśayaty ekaḥ
kṛtsnaṁ lokaṁ imam raviḥ /
kṣetraṁ kṣetrī tathā kṛtsnaṁ
prakāśayati Bhārata // 33

Just as the single sun illumines the whole universe, so the (one)

Indwelling Spirit enlivens all bodies (with self-consciousness).

Kṣetra-kṣetrajñāyor evam
antaraṁ jñāna-cakṣuṣā /
bhūta-prakṛti-mokṣaṁ ca
ye vidur yānti te param // 34

Whoever perceives by spiritual insight the distinction between Kṣetra (Nature) and Kṣetrajña (Spirit) as also the freedom of the Spirit from the hold of Nature, they reach the Supreme.

Chapter XIV

The Three Gunas

Śrī Bhagavān uvāca:

Paraṁ bhūyaḥ pravakṣyāmi
jñānānāṁ jñānam uttamam /
yaj jñātvā munayaḥ sarve
parāṁ siddhim ito gātāḥ // 1

The Blessed Lord said:

I shall now expound to you again that knowledge relating to the Supreme Being, the most exalted of all forms of knowledge, by gaining which all sages passed from this state of bondage into the highest perfection.

Idaṁ jñānam upāśritya
mama sādharmyam āgatāḥ /
sarge'pi n'opajāyante
pralaye na vyathanti ca // 2

Those who have attained unity with My nature through this knowledge are not born again even at the beginning of a new creative cycle, nor are they subjected to the distress of dissolution.

Mama yonir mahad brahma
tasmin garbhaṁ dadhāmy aham /
saṁbhavaḥ sarva-bhūtānāṁ
tato bhavati Bhārata // 3

The Great Nature Prakṛti is like a womb to Me. I deposit therein the germ of creation, the creative impulse, out of which everything comes into being.

Sarva-yoniṣu Kaunteya
mūrtayaḥ saṁbhavanti yāḥ /
tāsāṁ brahma mahad yonir
ahaṁ bīja-pradaḥ pitā // 4

O son of Kunti! All creatures, whatever might be the womb from which they are born, have really the Great Nature as the womb — the source of their origin. And I am their father, the bestower of the seed.

Sattvaṁ rajas tama iti
guṇāḥ prakṛti-saṁbhavāḥ /

nibadhnanti mahā-bāho
dehe dehinam avyayam // 5

The three Guṇas as Sattva, Rajas and Tamas born of Prakṛti, bind down the immortal soul to the body in its embodied state.

Tatra sattvaṁ nirmalatvāt
prakāśakam anāmayam /
sukha-saṅgena badhnāti
jñāna-sañgena c'ānagha // 6

Among these, Sattva is luminous and harmonious due to its essential purity. It binds the soul, O sinless one, with the feeling 'I am happy, I am full of knowledge.'

Rajo rāg'ātmakaṁ viddhi
tṛṣṇā-saṅga-samudbhavam /
tan nibadhnāti Kaunteya
karma-saṅgena dehinam // 7

Know Rajas to be passion-based, and productive of longings for unattained objects and attachment for those in one's possession. It binds the (actionless) soul, O son of Kunti, by entangling it in action through the feeling 'I am the doer.'

Tamas tu ajñāna-jaṁ viddhi
mohanaṁ sarva-dehinām /
pramād'ālasya-nidrābhis
tan nibadhnāti Bhārata // 8

As for the Guṇa known as Tamas, it is ignorance-born and is productive of delusion in all beings. It binds the soul, O scion of the Bhārata clan! with the obsession of a disposition characterised by negligence, indolence and sleepiness.

Sattvaṁ sukhe sañjayati
rajaḥ karmaṇi Bhārata /
jñānam āvṛtya tu tamaḥ
pramāde sañjayaty uta // 9

Sattva enslaves one to a mood of joy and happiness, and Rajas to one of activity, while Tamas, which veils up knowledge, fills one with negligence and laziness.

Rajas tamaś c'ābhibhūya
sattvaṁ bhavati Bhārata /
rajaḥ sattvaṁ tamaś c'aiva
tamaḥ sattvaṁ rajas tathā // 10

Overpowering Rajas and Tamas, Sattva prevails (sometimes); suppressing Sattva and Tamas, Rajas becomes dominant; and likewise dominating over Sattva and Rajas, Tamas holds the field.

Sarva-dvāreṣu dehe'smin
prakāśa upajāyate /
jñānaṁ yadā tadā vidyād
vivṛddhaṁ sattvam ity uta // 11

When through all the senses, which are the portals of the body, knowledge, happiness and similar characteristics manifest, then indeed it should be understood that Sattva is dominant.

Lobhaḥ pravṛttir-ārambhaḥ
karmaṇām aśamaḥ spṛhā /
rajasy etāni jāyante
vivṛddhe Bharatarṣabha // 12

Avarice, extroversion, ceaseless planning and execution of works, restlessness, desire for enjoyments — these arise when Rajas prevails.

Aprakāśo'pravṛttiś ca
pramādo moha eva ca /
tamasy etāni jāyante
vivṛddhe Kuru-nandana // 13

When Tamas dominates, there is lack of intelligence, lack of effort, negligence and delusion.

Yadā sattve pravṛddhe tu
pralayaṁ yāti deha-bhṛt /
tadottama-vidāṁ lokān
amalān pratipadyate // 14

If one dies when Sattva is prevailing dominant, then one attains to the pure regions of the knowers of the Highest.

Rajasi pralayaṁ gatvā
karma-saṅgiṣu jāyate /
tathā pralīnas tamasi
mūḍha-yoniṣu jāyate // 15

Those who die when Rajas dominates are born among those attached to action (men); and likewise those dying in Tamas are born in the wombs of creatures without reason (animals).

Karmaṇaḥ sukṛtasy'āhuḥ
sāttvikaṁ nirmalaṁ phalam /
rajasas tu phalaṁ duḥkham
ajñānaṁ tamasaḥ phalam // 16

Virtuous actions promote spirituality and purity (Sattva), while the Rajas-dominated ones result in pain, and the Tamas dominated ones in ignorance.

Sattvāt saṁjāyate jñānam
rajaso lobha eva ca /
pramāda-mohau tamaso
bhavato'jñānam eva ca // 17

From Sattva arises knowledge and from Rajas, avarice. Negligence. delusion and also ignorance are the products of Tamas.

Urdhvaṁ gacchanti sattva-sthā
madhye tiṣṭhanti rājasāḥ /
jaghanya-guṇa vṛtti-sthā
adho gacchanti tāmasāḥ // 18

Those established in Sattva evolve to higher goals, while those abiding in Rajas remain in the mid-course.

Steeped in evil tendencies, the Tamas-dominated ones degenerate.

N'ānyaṁ guṇebhyaḥ kartāraṁ
yadā draṣṭā'nupaśyati /
guṇebhyaś ca paraṁ vetti
mad-bhāvaṁ so'dhigacchati // 19

When the subject (Jīva) recognises the Guṇas alone as the agent in all actions, and himself as transcending the Guṇas — then he attains to My state.

Guṇān etān atītya trīn
dehī deha-samudbhavān /
janma-mṛtyu-jarā-duhkḥair
vimukto'mṛtam aśnute // 20

The embodied spirit (Jīva), having transcended the Guṇas from which the body has sprung, gains deliverance from the miseries of birth, death and old age, and attains to Immortality.

Arjuna uvāca:

Kair liṅgais trīn guṇān etān
atīto bhavati prabho /
kim-ācāraḥ kathaṁ c'aitāṁs
trīn guṇān ativartate // 21

Arjuna said:

Lord! What are the marks of one who has transcended these three Guṇas? How does he behave? And how does he rise above them?

Śrī Bhagavān uvāca:

Prakāśaṁ ca pravṛttiṁ ca
moham eva ca Pāṇḍava /
na dveṣṭi sampravṛttāni
na nivṛttāni kāṅkṣati // 22

The Blessed Lord said:

O son of Pāṇḍu! He who shows no aversion to knowledge,. activity, or delusion when any of them is dominant, nor longs for them when absent;

Udāsīnavad āsīno
guṇair yo na vicālyate /
guṇā vartanta ity eva
yo'vatiṣṭhati n'eṅgate // 23

Who remains like an unconcerned witness and is unperturbed by the Guṇa-born sense objects; who knows that it is only the Guṇa-born senses and mind that act and enjoy (and not his real self); who remains unwavering in all situations;

Sama-duḥkha-sukhaḥ svasthaḥ
sama-loṣṭāśma kāñcanaḥ /
tulya-priy'āpriyo dhīras
tulya-nind'ātma-saṁstutiḥ // 24

Who is self-poised alike in pleasure and in pain; who makes no difference between stone, iron, and gold; who is the same towards the loving and the hating; who is unmoved by praise and blame alike;

Mānāpamānayos tulyas
tulyo mitr'āri-pakkṣayoḥ /
sarv'āraṁbha-parityāgī
guṇ'ātītaḥ sa ucyate // 25

Who is alike in honour and in humiliation; who views a friend and a foe alike; who has abandoned all sense of agency — such a person is said to have transcended the Guṇas.

Māṁ ca yo'vyabhicāreṇa
bhakti-yogena sevate /
sa guṇān samatīty'aitān
brahma-bhūyāya kalpate // 26

He who serves Me through the communion of unswerving and exclusive devotion, transcends the Guṇas and attains fitness to become Brahman.

Brahmaṇo hi pratiṣṭhā'ham
amṛtasy'āvyayasya ca /
śāśvatasya ca dharmasya
sukhasy'aikāntikasya ca // 27

Indeed, I(Kṛṣṇa, the God of love and grace, or the Pratyagātman the true Inner Self), am the basic support of Brahman — of the incorruptible state of Mokṣa, of the Eternal Law and of unending Bliss.

Chapter XV

All-Pervading Divine Person

Śrī Bhagavān uvāca:

Ūrdhva-mūlam adhaḥ-śākham
aśvatthaṁ prāhur avyayam /
chandāṁsi yasya parṇāni
yas taṁ veda sa veda-vit // 1

The Blessed Lord said:

The scriptures speak of the eternal Aśvattha, the World Tree, whose roots are in the Most High, branches in the lower regions, and leaves in Vedic hymns. He who knows it, understands the Veda really.

Adhaś c'ordhvaṁ prasṛtās tasya śākhā
guṇa-pravṛddhā viṣaya-pravālāḥ /
adhaś ca mūlāny anusaṁtatāni
karm'ānubandhīni
manuṣya-loke // 2

Nourished by the Guṇas and covered with the budding foliage of sense objects, its branches spread into regions high and low. Stretching forth on the ground below in the world of men, are its secondary roots, entangling man in the bondage of action.

Na rūpam asy'eha tath'opalabhyate
n'ānto na c'ādir na ca saṁ-pratiṣṭhā /
aśvattham enaṁ suvirūḍha-mūlam
asaṅga-śastreṇa dṛḍhena chittvā //

Tataḥ padaṁ tat parimārgitavyaṁ
yasmin gatā ṅa nivartanti bhūyaḥ /
tam eva c'ādyaṁ puruṣaṁ prapadye
yataḥ pravṛttiḥ prasṛtā purāṇī // 3-4

For one involved in worldly life, the form of the World-Tree is not visible, nor its origin, nor its end, nor its foundation. Cutting asunder the firmly rooted Aśvattha (World-Tree) with the powerful axe of non-attachment, and saying, "I seek refuge in that Primeval Person from whom this eternal cosmic activity has streamed forth", man should seek that Status, attaining to which there is no more return to this life of Saṁsāra.

Nirmāna-mohā-jita-saṅga-doṣā
adhyātma-nityā vinivṛtta-kāmāḥ /
dvandvair vimuktāḥ
sukha-duḥkha-samjñair
gacchanty amūḍhāḥ padam
avyayaṁ tat // 5

They who are free from pride and delusion, who have no attachments, who are ever absorbed in spritual pursuits, who are free from all worldly desires, who are unaffected by the varying situations of pleasurable and painful nature — such persons, freed from ignorance, attain to the Eternal State.

Na tad bhāsayate sūryo
na śaśāṅko na pāvakaḥ /
yad gatvā na nivartante
tad dhāma paramaṁ mama // 6

That the sun does not illumine, nor the moon, nor the fire; (for it is the Light of Pure Consciousness). Having attained It, the Spirit does not return again to the life of Saṁsāra. Such is My Supreme Abode.

Mam'aiv'āṁśo jīva-loke
jīva-bhūtaḥ sanātanaḥ /

manaḥ-ṣaṣṭhānī'ndriyāṇi
prakṛti-sthāni karṣati // 7

A fragment of Myself, immortal in nature, having become the embodied spirit in the world of the living, attracts to Himself the mind and the five senses born of Prakṛti.

Śarīraṁ yad avāpnoti
yac c'āpy utkrāmat'īśvaraḥ /
gṛhītv'aitāni saṁyāti
vāyur gandhān iv'āśayāt // 8

When he gets a new body or abandons an old one, the Jīva, the lord of the body, moves, carrying them (the mind and the senses) with him, as the wind carries smells from their seats (in flowers and the like).

Śrotraṁ cakṣuḥ sparśanaṁ ca
rasanaṁ ghrāṇam eva ca /
adhiṣṭhāya manaś c'āyaṁ
viṣayān upasevate // 9

In identification with the senses like hearing, sight, touch, taste and smell, this Jīva experiences their respective objects.

Utkrāmantaṁ sthitaṁ vā'pi
bhunjānaṁ vā guṇ'ānvitam /
vimūḍhā n'ānupaśyanti
paśyanti jñāna-cakṣuṣaḥ // 10

The deluded do not recognise the Spirit (Jīva) when, in identification with the Guṇas, he tenates or leaves a body, or when he experiences objects through it; but those endowed with the eye of wisdom do.

Yatanto yoginaś c'ainaṁ
paśyanty ātmany avasthitam /
yatanto'py akṛt'ātmāno
n'ainaṁ paśyanty acetasaḥ // 11

The striving contemplatives perceive the Ātman within themselves, but not the impure and the unregenerate, though they be striving.

Yad āditya-gataṁ tejo
jagad bhāsayate'khilam /
yac candramasi yac c'āgnau
tat tejo viddhi māmakam // 12

That light of the sun which illumines the whole universe, which is present in the moon and in fire likewise — know that splendour to be Mine.

Gām āviśya ca bhūtāni
dhārayāmy aham ojasā /
puṣṇāmi c'auṣadhīḥ sarvāḥ
somo bhūtvā ras'ātmakaḥ // 13

Entering the earth by My spiritual energy, I sustain all beings residing in it. As the watery moon, I nourish all herbs.

Ahaṁ vaiśvānaro bhūtvā
prāṇināṁ deham āśritaḥ /
prāṇ'āpāna-samāyuktaḥ
pacāmy annaṁ catur-vidham // 14

Based in the body of living beings, I manifest as the digestive Fire, Vaiśvānara, and in combination with the vital energies known as Prāṇa and Apāna, digest the four kinds of food taken by them.

Sarvasya c'āhaṁ hṛdi saṁniviṣṭo
mattaḥ smṛtir jñānam apohanaṁ ca /
vedaiś ca sarvair aham eva vedyo
vedānta-kṛd veda-vid
eva c'āham // 15

I abide in the hearts of all. By My will both the dawn and effacement of memory (of past births) and of supersensuous knowledge take place. The original teacher of the Vedanta I am, as also the knower of all Vedas.

Dvāv imau puruṣau loke
kṣaraś c'ākṣara eva ca /
kṣaraḥ sarvāṇi bhūtani
kūta-stho'kṣara ucyate // 16

It is well known that there are two types of Puruṣas (spirits or categories) — the Kṣara or the Perishable and Akṣara, the Imperishable. The Kṣara consists of all the Jīvas in embodiment who are subject to change, while the Akṣara consists of the collectivity of liberated Jīvas who remain aloof from changeful matter and are unaffected by it; (or in the alternative, the Creative Power Māyā-śakti, which is the source of all falsity and the cause of endless Saṁsāra).

Uttamaḥ puruṣas tu anyaḥ
param'ātm'ety udāhṛtaḥ /
yo loka-trayam āviśya
bibharty avyaya iśvaraḥ // 17

But there is yet another Puruṣa, known as the Supreme Being or the Puruṣottama, who is the highest of spirits, and who pervades all the three worlds and sustains them.

Yasmāt kṣaram atīto'ham
akṣarād api c'ottamaḥ /
ato'smi loke vede ca
prathitaḥ puruṣ'ottamaḥ // 18

As I transcend the Perishable and am also superior to the Imperishable, I am well-known as the Puruṣottama (the Supreme Being) in both the Vedic and secular literature.

Yo mām evam asammūḍho
jānāti puruṣ'ottamam /
sa sarvavid bhajati māṁ
sarva bhāvena bhārata // 19

He who knows Me in this way as the Puruṣottama, he understands the true nature of this Totality, and he loves and adores Me with his whole being.

Iti guhyatamaṁ śāstram
idam uktaṁ mayā'nagha /
etad buddhvā buddhimān syāt
kṛta-kṛtyaś ca Bhārata // 20

O sinless one! This spiritual doctrine, the most profound of all in the sacred lore, has now been revealed by Me. A true understanding of it makes a man really wise and established in a sense of total fulfilment.

Chapter XVI

Divine and Demoniac Types

Śrī Bhagavān uvāca:

Abhayaṁ sattva-saṁśuddhir
jñāna-yoga-vyavasthitiḥ /
dānaṁ damaś ca yajñas ca
svādhyāyas tapa ārjavam // 1

The Blessed Lord said:

Fearlessness, purity of heart, steadfastness in knowledge and devotion, benevolence, control of the senses, worship, study of scriptures, austerity, uprightness;

Ahiṁsā satyam akrodhas
tyāgaḥ śāntir apaiśunam /
dayā bhūteṣu aloluptvaṁ
mārdavaṁ hrīr acāpalam // 2

Non-violence, truthfulness, freedom from anger, renunciation, tranquillity, aversion to slander, compassion to living beings, freedom from sensuality, gentleness, modesty, steadfastness;

Tejaḥ kṣamā dhṛtiḥ śaucam
adroho n'ātimānitā /
bhavanti saṁpadaṁ daivīm
abhijātasya Bhārata // 3

Vigour, patience, fortitdude, harmlessness, freedom from vanity—

all these, O scion of the Bharatas, are present in those born to a divine heritage.

Dambho darpo'bhimānaś ca
krodhaḥ pāruṣyam eva ca /
ajñānaṁ c'ābhijātasya
Pārtha saṁpadam āsurīṁ // 4

O son of Pṛthā! Pretentiousness, arrogance, overweening pride, wrath, rudeness, as also insensitiveness to spiritual values — all these are found in those born to a demoniac heritage.

Daivī saṁpad vimokṣāya
nibandhāy'āsurī matā /
mā śucaḥ saṁpadaṁ daivīm
abhijāto'si Pāṇḍava // 5

It is deemed that the divine heritage leads to liberation and the demoniac to bondage. Grieve not, O son of Pāṇḍu! You are born to a divine heritage.

Dvau bhūta-sargau loke'smin
daiva āsura eva ca /
daivo vistaraśaḥ prokta
āsuraṁ Pārtha me śṛṇu // 6

In this world there are two types of creation, the divine and the demoniac. The divine heritage has already been described. Now hear from Me what constitutes the demoniac heritage, O son of Pṛthā.

Pravṛttiṁ ca nivṛttiṁ ca
janā na vidur āsurāḥ /

na śaucaṁ nā'pi c'ācāro
na satyaṁ teṣu vidyate // 7

Men of demoniac nature know not what should be done and what should be avoided. Neither purity, nor good conduct, nor truthfulness is found in them.

Asatyam apratiṣṭhaṁ te
jagad āhur anīśvaram /
aparaspara-sambhūtaṁ
kim anyat kāma-haitukam // 8

According to them nothing is ultimately real in this world. It is Godless and without any moral basis. Being born of sexual union, what else but lust can be said to be its cause?

Etāṁ dṛṣṭim avaṣṭabhya
naṣṭ'ātmāno'lpa-buddhayaḥ /
prabhavanty ugra-karmāṇaḥ
kṣayāya jagato'hitāḥ // 9

Holding such views, these lost souls — these men of little understanding — given, as they are, to cruel deeds opposed to general well-being, appear as agents for the destruction of the world.

Kāmam āśritya duṣpūraṁ
daṁbha-māna-mad'ānvitāḥ /
mohād gṛhitvā'sad-grāhān
pravartante'śuci-vratāḥ // 10

Steeped in insatiable lust, motivated by hypocrisy, vanity, arrogance and avarice, given to corrupt and impure ways of life, they work in pursuit of false values entertained through delusion.

Cintām aparimeyāṁ ca
pralay'āntām upāśritāḥ /
kām'opabhoga-paramā
etāvad iti niścitāḥ // 11

Obsessed with numerous cares all through life, looking on sex indulgence as the highest aim, convinced that there is no higher purpose in life than this;

Āśā-pāśa-śatair baddhāḥ
kāma-krodha-parāyaṇāḥ /
īhante kāma-bhog'ārtham
anyāyen'ārtha-sañcayān // 12

Bound with a hundred cords of hopes and expectations, and enslaved by lust and anger, they strive to accumulate wealth in improper ways for the fulfilment of their sensuous desires.

Idam adya mayā labdham
imaṁ prāpsye manoratham /
idam ast'īdam api me
bhaviṣyati punar dhanam // 13

"Today I have gained this object, tomorrow I shall gain that object of desire too; I have this much wealth now, much more will be mine hereafter;

Asau mayā hataḥ śatrur
haniṣye cā'parān api /
īśvaro'haṁ aham bhogī
siddho'haṁ balavān sukhī // 14

"This enemy has been slain, the others too I will soon destroy; I am the master; everything is for my enjoyment; I am the successful man, the powerful man, the happy man;

Āḍhyo'bhijanavān asmi
ko'nyo'sti sadṛśo mayā /

yakṣye dāsyāmi modiṣya
ity ajñāna-vimohitāḥ // 15

"I am wealthy and high-born; who is there like unto me? I will perform sacrifices, I will make charity, and I will rejoice" — deluded thus by ignorance;

Aneka-citta-vibhrāntā
moha-jāla-samāvṛtāḥ /
prasaktāḥ kāma-bhogeṣu
patanti narake'śucau // 16

Gripped by numerous bewildering thoughts, entangled in the meshes of delusion, and ever given to sex indulgences, they are degraded into states that are loathsome and full of suffering.

Ātma-saṁbhāvitāḥ stabdhā-
dhana-māna-mad'ānvitāḥ /
yajante nāma-yajñais te
daṁbhen'āvidhipūrvakam // 17

Vain-glorious, stubborn and intoxicated with the pride of wealth, they perform for mere show Yajñas that are so in name only, being done without the observance of the commandments of the scriptures.

Ahaṁkāraṁ balaṁ darpaṁ
kāmaṁ krodhaṁ ca saṁśritāḥ /
māṁ ātma-para-deheṣu
pradviṣanto'bhyasūyakāḥ // 18

Dominated by self-conceit, prone to the use of force, arrogant, lustful and choleric, these traducers of virtue violate Me, dwelling in them and also in others.

Tān ahaṁ dviṣataḥ krūrān
saṁsāreṣu nar'ādhamān /
kṣipāmy ajasram aśubhān
āsurīṣveva yoniṣu // 19

These vicious men, oppressive cruel and sinful as they are, — are always hurled down by Me into demoniac wombs in life after life in the transmigratory cycle.

Āsurīṁ yonim āpannā
mūḍhā janmani janmani /

mām aprāpy'aiva Kaunteya
tato yānty adhamāṁ gatim // 20

O son of Kunti! Falling into demoniac wombs, in life after life, they go to still lower states of degradation, without attaining Me.

Tri-vidhaṁ narakasy'edaṁ
dvāraṁ nāśanam ātmanaḥ /
kāmaḥ krodhas-tathā lobhas
tasmād etat trayaṁ tyajet // 21

Lust, anger and greed — this triad leads to the destruction of man's spiritual nature. They form the gateway to hell; they should be abandoned.

Etair vimuktaḥ Kaunteya
tamo-dvārais tribhir naraḥ /
ācaraty ātmanaḥ śreyas
tato yāti parāṁ gatim // 22

If a man is free from these three, the gateways to hell, he can work out his own good and reach the highest goal.

Yaḥ śāstra-vidhim utsṛjya
vartate kāma-kārataḥ /
na sa siddhim avāpnoṭi
na sukhaṁ na parāṁ gatim // 23

He who abandons the commandments of the scriptures and lives as his desires prompt him, he attains neither spiritual perfection, nor worldly happiness nor liberation.

Tasmāc chāstraṁ pramāṇaṁ te
kāry'ākārya-vyavasthitau /
jñātvā śāstra-vidhān'oktaṁ
karma kartum ihā'rhasi // 24

Therefore let the scriptures be your norm in determining what should be done and what not. Understand the injunction of the scriptures first and then set yourself to work.

Chapter XVII

Three Aspects of Faith

Arjuna uvāca:

Ye śāstra-vidhim utsṛjya
yajante śraddhayā'nvitāḥ /
teṣāṁ niṣṭhā tu kā Kṛṣṇa
sattvam āho rajas tamaḥ // 1

Arjuna said:

There are persons who offer worship full of Faith, but without observing scriptural injunctions while doing so — of what nature is their Faith? Is it born of Sattva, Rajas or Tamas?

Śrī Bhagavān uvāca:

Tri-vidhā bhavati śraddhā
dehināṁ sā svabhāva -jā /
sāttvikī rājasī c'aiva
tāmasī c'eti tāṁ ṣṛṇu // 2

The Blessed Lord said:

The Faith of embodied beings, which is rooted in their natural disposition (derived from the impressions of past births), is of three kinds — those of the nature of Sattva, of Rajas and of Tamas.

Sattv'ānurūpā sarvasya
śraddhā bhavati Bhārata /

śraddhāmayo'yaṁ puruṣo
yo yac-chraddaḥ sa eva saḥ // 3

O scion of the Bharata race! The Faith of everyone is according to his natural disposition (derived from past impressions). Man is constituted of his Faith. What his Faith is, that verily he is.

Yajante sāttvikā devān
yakṣa-rakṣāṁsi rājasāḥ /
pretān bhūta-gaṇāṁś c'ānye
yajante tāmasā janāḥ // 4

Those endowed with the quality of Sattva worship the Devas; those with Rajas, the Yakṣas and the Rākṣasas;

and those with Tamas, the spirits of dead ancestors and the elementals.

Aśāstra-vihitaṁ ghoraṁ
tapyante ye tapo janāḥ /
daṁbh'ā haṁkāra-saṁyuktāḥ
kāma-rāga-balānvitāḥ //

karṣayantaḥ śarīra-sthaṁ
bhūta-grāmam acetasaḥ /
māṁ c'aivā'ntaḥ-śarīra-sthaṁ
tān viddhy āsura-niścayān // 5-6

Vain, conceited and moved by powerful passions and attachments, they perform various terrible mortifications contrary to scriptural injunctions. Thus do these senseless men torture their own bodies and Me dwelling in them. Know such persons to be of demoniac resolve.

Āhāras as ty api sarvasya
tri-vidho bhavati priyaḥ /
yajñas-tapas-tathā dānaṁ
teṣām bhedaṁ imaṁ ṣṛṇu // 7

Even the food dear to these three types is of three different kinds. The same is the case with worship, austerity and charity. Hear from Me about this distinction regarding them.

Āyuḥ-sattva-bal'ārogya
sukha-prīti-vivardhanāḥ /
rasyāḥ snigdhāḥ sthirā hṛdyā
āhārāḥ sāttvika-priyāḥ // 8

Persons who are Sāttvika by nature like foods that promote longevity, vitality, energy, health, happiness and cheerfulness, as also those that are juicy, soft, nourishing and agreeable.

Kaṭv-amla-lavaṇ'ātyuṣṇa
tīkṣṇa-rūkṣa-vidāhinaḥ /
āhārā rājasasy'eṣṭā
duḥkha-śok'āmaya-pradāḥ // 9

Persons who are Rājasa by nature like foods that are bitter, sour, salty, excessively heating, pungent, burning and thirst-producing as also what bring on uneasiness, depression and disease.

Yātayāmaṁ gatarasaṁ
pūti paryuṣitaṁ ca yat /
ucchiṣṭam api cā'medhyaṁ
bhojanaṁ tāmasa-priyam // 10

Persons who are Tāmasa by nature like foods that are stale, tasteless, putrid, decayed and unclean, and constitute the leavings of others.

Aphal'ākāṅkṣibhir yajño
vidhī-dṛṣṭo ya ijyate /
yaṣṭavyam ev'eti manaḥ
samādhāya sa sāttvikaḥ // 11

That worship is of the nature of Sattva which is in accordance with scriptural injunctions, and which is performed by one not with an eye for its fruits but merely out of the feeling that it is one's duty to perform it.

Abhisaṁdhāya tu phalaṁ
daṁbh'ārtham api c'aiva yat /
ijyate bharata-śreṣṭha
taṁ yajñaṁ viddhi rājasam // 12

O scion of the Bharata race! Know that worship to be of the nature of Rajas, which is performed with its fruits in mind and for vain display.

Vidhihīnam asṛṣṭ'ānnaṁ
mantra-hīnam adakṣiṇam /
śraddhā-virahitaṁ yajñaṁ
tāmasaṁ paricakṣate // 13

That worship is of the nature of Tamas which is not sanctioned by scriptures, which is without gift of food, without the chanting of holy Mantras, without sacramental presents and without sincere faith.

Deva-dvija-guru-prājña
pūjanaṁ śaucam ārjavam /
brahmacaryam ahimsā ca
śārīraṁ tapa ucyate // 14

Service of the Devas, holy men, teachers, parents and wise persons, as also observance of cleanliness, uprightness, continence and non-injury — these constitute austerities pertaining to the body.

Anudvega-karaṁ vākyaṁ
satyaṁ priya-hitaṁ ca yat /
svādhyāy'ābhyasanaṁ c'aiva
vāṅmayaṁ tapa ucyate // 15

Speaking only words that are inoffensive, true, pleasant and beneficial, as also regular recitation of scriptures, constitute austerity pertaining to speech.

Manaḥ-prasādaḥ saumyatvaṁ
maunam ātma-vinigrahaḥ /
bhāva-saṁśuddhir ity-etat
tapo mānasam ucyate // 16

Serenity of mind, gentleness, moderation in speech, self-control, and purity of heart — these are called austerity of the mind.

Śraddhayā parayā taptaṁ
tapas tat trividhaṁ naraḥ /
aphal'ākāṅkṣibhir-yuktaiḥ
sāttvikaṁ paricakṣate // 17

This threefold austerity, performed with the highest faith, by men who are not motivated by expectations of reward and who are established in mental equipoise, is declared to be of the nature of Sattva.

Satkāra-māna-pūj'ārthaṁ
tapo daṁbhena c'aiva yat /
kriyate tad iha proktaṁ
rājasaṁ calam adhṛuvam // 18

The austerity that is performed with much show and ostentation, and having in view recognition, praise and adoration as a pious man by others, is said to be of the nature of Rajas. It is unstable and leads to no permanent good.

Mūḍha-grāheṇ'ātmano yat
pīḍayā kriyate tapaḥ /
parasyotsādan'ārthaṁ vā
tat tāmasam udāhṛtam // 19

The austerity performed through the practice of self-torture under the influence of perverse theories or done for the destruction of another, is spoken of as Tamasa by nature.

Dātavyam iti yad dānaṁ
dīyate'nupakāriṇe /
deśe kāle ca pātre ca
tad dānaṁ sāttvikaṁ smṛtam // 20

That gift which is made out of a sheer sense of duty, without expectation of any kind of return, at the proper time and place, to a fit recipient, is said to be of the nature of Sattva.

Yat tu pratyupakār'ārthaṁ
phalam uddiśya vā punaḥ /
dīyate ca parikliṣṭaṁ
tad dānaṁ rājasaṁ smṛtam // 21

The gift which is given in consideration of some gift in return, or with some fruit to be reaped in future, or in a grudging mood — that is considered to be of the nature of Rajas.

Adeśa-kāle yad dānam
apātrebhyaś ca dīyate /
asatkṛtam avajñātaṁ
tat tāmasam udāhṛtam // 22

The gift that is made at an improper time and place, to an unworthy recipient, unceremoniously and in a slighting manner — that is said to be of the nature of Tamas.

Om tat sad iti nirdeśo
brahmaṇas-tri-vidhaḥ smṛtaḥ /

brāhmaṇās tena vedāś ca
yajñāś ca vihitāḥ purā // 23

Om Tat Sat — these are the three symbolic designations of Brahman. By these were ordained the Brāhmaṇas, the Vedas and the Yajñas in ancient times.

Tasmād om ity udāhṛtya
yajña-dāna-tapaḥ-kriyāḥ /
pravartante vidhān'oktāḥ
satataṁ brahma-vādinām // 24

Therefore the followers of the Vedas always start their ordained works like sacrifice, gift, and austerities with the utterance of Om.

Tad ity anabhisaṁdhāya
phalaṁ yajña-tapaḥ-kriyāḥ /
dāna-kriyāś ca vividhāḥ
kriyante mokṣa-kāṅkṣibhiḥ // 25

Various forms of sacrifices, austerities and charities are performed without any desire for the fruits by seekers after liberation, along with the utterance of the syallable Tat (That).

Sad-bhāve sādhu-bhāve ca
sad ity etat prayujyate /
praśaste karmaṇi tathā
sac-chabdaḥ Pārtha yujyate // 26

O son of Pṛthā! The syllable Sat is used in the sense of reality and goodness. It is also used to indicate an auspicious rite or act.

Yajñe tapasi dāne ca
sthitiḥ sad iti c'ocyate /
karma c'aiva tad-arthīyaṁ
sad ity ev'ābhidhīyate // 27

Steadfastness in sacrifice (or worship), in austerity and in charity is called Sat (good). Any action connected with these is also called Sat.

Aśraddhayā hutaṁ dattaṁ
tapas taptaṁ kṛtaṁ ca yat /
asad ity ucyate Pārtha
na ca tat pretya no iha // 28

O son of Pṛthā! Whatever is performed as a sacrifice, charity, or austerity without Faith — in fact anything done without Faith — is declared to be Asat (not good). It is of no significance here or in the hereafter.

Chapter XVIII

Liberation Through Renunciation

Arjuna uvāca:

Saṁnyāsasyā mahā-bāho
tattvam icchāmi veditum /
tyāgasya ca Hṛṣīkeśa
pṛthak Keśi-niṣūdana // 1

Arjuna said:

O mighty-armed One, famed as the destroyer of Keśin and the conqueror of the senses! I desire to know the true nature of Saṁnyāsa, and as distinguished from it, of Tyāga too.

Śrī Bhagavān uvāca:

Kāmyānāṁ karmaṇāṁ nyāsaṁ
saṁnyāsaṁ kavayo viduḥ /
sarva-karma-phala-tyāgaṁ
prāhus tyāgaṁ vicakṣaṇāḥ // 2

Abandonment of all desire-prompted actions is Saṁnyāsa (renunciation) according to the wise. Men of discernment speak of the abandonment of the fruits of all actions as Tyāga (relinquishment).

Tyājyaṁ doṣavad ity eke
karma prāhur manīṣiṇaḥ /
yajña-dāna-tapaḥ-karma
na tyājyam iti c'āpare // 3

Some wise men say that all action is to be abandoned as evil. Others maintain that good works like worship, charity and practice of austerity are not to be abandoned.

Niścayaṁ sṛṇu me tatra
tyāge Bharata-sattama /
tyago hi puruṣa-vyāghra
tri-vidhaḥ saṁprakīrtitaḥ // 4

O the best of the Bhārata race! Hear my conclusive view on this subject of Tyāga (relinquishment). It is said that there are three types of Tyāga.

Yajña-dāna-tapaḥ-karma
na tyājyaṁ kāryam eva tat /

yajño dānaṁ tapaśc'aiva
pāvanāni manīṣiṇām // 5

Works like sacrifice, charity and austerity should not be abandoned. They should be performed; for sacrifice, charity and austerity are indeed purifying for the wise.

Etāny api tu karmāṇi
saṅgaṁ tyaktvā phalāni ca /
kartavyānī'ti me Pārtha
niścitaṁ matam uttamam // 6

O Son of Pṛthā! Even these works are to be performed without attachment and desire for their fruits. This is My settled and decisive view.

Niyatasya tu saṁnyāsaḥ
karmaṇo n'opapadyate /
mohāt tasya parityāgas
tāmasaḥ parikīrtitaḥ // 7

It is not at all proper to renounce works that ought to be done as duty. Their abandonment out of delusion is considered to be of the nature of Tamas.

Duḥkham ity eva yat karma
kāya-kleśa-bhayāt tyajet /
sa kṛtvā rājasaṁ tyāgaṁ
n'aiva tyāga-phalaṁ labhet // 8

Those who give up work out of a dread of physical suffering, out of a feeling that it is painful, they, performing relinquishment of a Rājasa nature, do not obtain the results of true relinquishment.

Kāryam ity eva yat karma
niyataṁ kriyate'rjuna /
Saṅgaṁ tyaktvā phalaṁ c'aiva
sa tyāgaḥ sāttviko mataḥ // 9

But, O Arjuna! That relinquishment is considered as Sāttvika which consists in giving up attachment and thoughts of returns in respect of works, and which is done with the feeling that it is an obligatory duty that must necessarily be performed.

Na dveṣṭy akuśalaṁ karma
kuśale n'ānuṣajjate /
tyāgi sattva-samāviṣṭo
medhāvī chinna-saṁśayaḥ // 10

The relinquisher (Tyāgī), if he is endowed with the qualities of Sattva, wisdom and conviction in regard to the spiritual ideal, never avoids duties merely because they are unpleasant, nor does he get attached to works that seem pleasant to him.

Na hi deha-bhṛtā śakyaṁ
tyaktuṁ karmāṇy aśeṣataḥ /
yas tu karma-phala-tyāgī
sa tyagī'ty abdhidhīyate // 11

It is not indeed possible for any embodied being (i.e., one with body-consciousness) to abandon works in entirety. So all that one can do is to abandon the fruits of action. One doing so is called a Tyāgī (a relinquisher).

Aniṣṭam iṣṭaṁ miśraṁ ca
tri-vidhaṁ karmaṇaḥ phalam /
bhavaty atyāginām pretya
na tu saṁnyāsinām kvacit // 12

Regarding those who have not relinquished their desires (*atyāginām*), they reap after death the fruits of their actions performed with desire. They are of three sorts —

'unpleasant' like degradation into animal life or stay in purgatory for the very wicked; 'pleasant' like attainment of heavenly felicities for the virtuous; and mixed' as in human birth, for those who have Karmas of both these types to their credit. But Samnyasins (true renouncers) will have none of these.

Pañc'aitāni mahā-bāho
kāraṇani nibodha me /
sāṁkhye kṛtānte proktāni
siddhaye sarva-karmaṇām // 13

Learn from me, O mighty armed! about the five causal factors required for all actions as described in the

Sāṁkhya, the philosophy of spiritual illumination, which is the ultimate purpose of all actions.

Adhiṣṭhānaṁ tathā kartā
karaṇaṁ ca pṛthag-vidham /
vividhāś ca pṛthak-ceṣṭā
daivaṁ c'aiv'ātra pañcamam // 14

One's body which is the seat of action, the ego claiming to be the actor, the several instruments of actions (like the senses, the mind etc.), the varied and the distinct types of movements involved, and finally the unknown factor (or the deities presiding over the senses) as the fifth — these are the five causal factors.

Śarīra-vāṅ-manobhir yat
karma prārabhate naraḥ /
nyāyyaṁ vā viparītaṁ vā
pañc'aite tasya hetavaḥ // 15

These are the five causal factors involved in all actions, good as also bad, which men undertake with this body, speech and mind.

Tatr'aivaṁ sati kartāram
ātmānaṁ kevalaṁ tu yaḥ /
paśyaty akṛta-buddhitvān
na sa paśyati durmatiḥ // 16

That being so, he whose imperfect understanding makes him think that the self alone (or the unlimited and unrelated Ātman) is the agent involved in work — he verily sees not, being perverted in outlook.

Yasya n'āhaṁkṛto bhāvo
buddhir yasya na lipyate /
hattvā'pi sa imāṁl lokān
na hanti na nibadhyate // 17

He who is ever established in the feeling 'I am not the agent' and whose mind is consequently unsullied by attachments — he kills not really, nor is he bound, even though he annihilates all these beings.

Jñānaṁ jñeyaṁ parijñātā
tri-vidhā karma-codanā /

karaṇaṁ karma kart'eti
tri-vidhaḥ karma-saṁgrahaḥ // 18

Knowledge, object of knowledge, and knower — these constitute the threefold incitement to action. And the three constituents of action are the instruments of action, the purpose of action, and the agent.

Jñānaṁ karma ca kartā ca
tridh'aiva guṇa-bhedataḥ /
procyate guṇa-saṁkhyāne
yathāvac chṛṇu tānyapi // 19

In the philosophy dealing with the Guṇas and their evolutes, knowledge, action and agent are each divided into three according to the preponderance of each Guṇa in them. Hear of them also as they are.

Sarva-bhūteṣu yen'aikaṁ
bhāvam avyayam īkṣate /
avibhaktaṁ vibhakteṣu
taj jñānaṁ viddhi sāttvikam // 20

That knowledge by which one is able to see a unitary unmodifiable Essence, undivided among the divided, — know that knowledge to be of the nature of Sattva.

Pṛthaktvena tu yaj jñānaṁ
nānā-bhāvān pṛthag-vidhān /
vetti sarveṣu bhūteṣu
taj jñānaṁ viddhi rājasam // 21

That knowledge which apprehends all beings as a multiplicity with mutual distinction and in their separateness only, without any apprehension of an underlying unity — know that knowledge to be born of Rajas.

Yat tu kṛtsnavad ekasmin
kārye saktam ahaitukam /
atattv'ārthavad alpaṁ ca
tat tāmasam udāhṛtam // 22

That by which one dogmatically holds on to a part as if it were the whole (or looks on the body, an effect, as the whole man) — a view which is irrational, untrue and silly — that knowledge is said to be born of Tamas.

Niyataṁ saṅga-rahitam
arāga-dveṣataḥ kṛtam /
aphala-prepsunā karma
yat tat sāttvikam ucyate // 23

Work of the nature of duty done by one without hankering for fruits, and without attachment, or passion or hate — such work is spoken of as born of Sattva.

Yat tu kām'epsunā karma
s'āhaṁkāreṇa vā punaḥ /
kriyate bahul'āyāsaṁ
tad rājasam udāhṛtam // 24

But work that is done by a person merely for the gratification of his desire, and with great strain and a feeling of self-importance is said to be born of Rajas.

Anubandhaṁ kṣayaṁ hiṁsām
anapekṣya ca pauruṣam /
mohād ārabhyate karma
yat tat tāmasam ucyate // 25

And that work which is performed under delusion, without any regard to consequences, loss, injury to others, and to one's own capacity — is said to be born of Tamas.

Mukta-saṅgo'nahaṁ-vādī
dhṛty-utsāha-samanvitaḥ /

siddhy-asiddhyor nirvikāraḥ
kartā sāttvika ucyate // 26

A 'doer' (an agent of an action) who is without any attachment and sense of pride and self-importance, who is endowed with steadiness and zeal, and who is unruffled in success and failure — such a doer is said to be of the nature of Sattva.

Rāgī karma-phala-prepsur
lubdho hims'ātmako'śuciḥ /
harṣa-śok'ānvitaḥ kartā
rājasaḥ parikīrtitaḥ // 27

A 'doer' who is swayed by passion, who is keen on the fruits of his actions, who is covetous, cruel and impure at heart, and who is subject to elation and depression in success and failure — such a doer is said to be of the nature of Rajas.

Ayuktaḥ prākṛtaḥ stabdhaḥ
śaṭho naikṛtiko'lasaḥ /
viṣādī dīrgha-sūtrī ca
kartā tāmasa ucyate // 28

And a 'doer' who is unsteady, vulgar, arrogant, deceitful, malicious, indolent, despondent, and procrastinating — such a doer is said to be of the nature of Tamas.

Buddher bhedaṁ dhṛteś'caiva
guṇatas tri-vidhaṁ śṛṇu /

procyamānam aśeṣeṇa
pṛthaktvena dhanañjaya // 29

Hear now, O Arjuna, of the threefold division of the intellect and of the power of determination on the basis of their constituent Guṇas — hear of them severally and in their totality.

Pravṛttiṁ ca nivṛttiṁ ca
kāry'ākārye bhay'ābhaye /
bandhaṁ mokṣaṁ ca yā vetti
buddhiḥ sā Pārtha sāttvikī // 30

O son of Pṛthā! That intellect is said to be of the nature of Sattva which grasps the distinction between worldliness and renunciation, between the moral and the immoral, between what should be feared and what should not be, and between knowledge and freedom.

Yayā dharmam adharmaṁ ca
kāryaṁ c'ākāryam eva ca
ayathāvat prajānāti
buddhiḥ sā Pārtha rājasī // 31

O son of Pṛthā! That intellect is said to be of the nature of Rajas, which takes a distorted and confused view of the moral and the immoral, of what should be done and what should not be.

Adharmaṁ dharmam iti yā
manyate tamasā'vṛtā /
sarv'ārthān viparītāṁś ca
buddhiḥ sā Pārtha tāmasī // 32

O son of Pṛthā! That intellect is of the nature of Tamas, which, covered by the darkness of ignorance, understands the immoral as the moral and thus reverses all values.

Dhṛtyā yayā dhārayate
manaḥ-prāṇ'endriya-kriyāḥ /
yogen'āvyabhicāriṇyā
dhṛtiḥ sā Pārtha sāttvikī // 33

O Son of Pṛthā! That power of determination is of the nature of Sattva, by which the mind, the vital energy and the senses are held in control through unswerving concentration.

Yayā tu dharma-kām'ārthān
dhṛtyā dhārayate'rjuna /
prasaṅgena phal'ākāṅkṣī
dhṛtiḥ sā Pārtha rājasī // 34

That power of determination is of the nature of Rajas, by which one holds on to duty, pleasure and wealth with passionate attachment, motivated by the desire for their fruits.

Yayā svapnaṁ bhayaṁ śokaṁ
viṣādaṁ madam eva ca /
na vimuñcati durmedhā
dhṛtiḥ sā Pārtha tāmasī // 35

That power of determination is of the nature of Tamas, due to which one of perverted intelligence does not give up sloth, fear, grief, despondency and frenzy of sense indulgences.

Sukhaṁ tu idānīṁ tri-vidhaṁ
śṛṇu me Bharata'rṣabha /
abhyāsād ramate yatra
duḥkh'āntaṁ ca nigacchati //

Yat tad agre viṣam iva
pariṇāme'mṛt'opamam /
tat sukhaṁ sāttvikaṁ proktam
ātma-buddhi-prasāda-jam // 36-37

Hear from Me now about the three kinds of pleasures, O the greatest of the Bharata clan! That pleasure is said to be of the nature of Sattva which is gained by long practice of disciplines, which puts an end to all sorrows that man is heir to, which is like poison in the beginning but nectar-like at the end, and which springs from the serenity arising from the consciousness of the Ātman.

Viṣay'endriya-saṁyogād
yat tad agre'mṛt'opamam /
pariṇāme viṣam iva
tat sukhaṁ rājasaṁ smṛtam // 38

That pleasure is declared to be of the nature of Rajas, which is born of the union of the senses with their objects, which seems nectar-like in the beginning but turns to be poison in the end.

Yad agre c'ānubandhe ca
sukhaṁ mohanam ātmanaḥ /
nidr'ālasya-pramād'otthaṁ
tat tāmasam udāhṛtam // 39

That pleasure is of the nature of Tamas, which springs from sleepiness, sloth and heedlessness, and which is delusive in its effect on the spirit from beginning to end.

Na tad asti pṛthivyāṁ vā
divi deveṣu vā punaḥ /
sattvaṁ prakṛtijair muktaṁ
yad ebhiḥ syāt tribhir guṇaiḥ // 40

Nowhere, be it in this world or in the heavenly regions of the Devas, is there any being who is free from these three Guṇas of Nature (Prakṛti).

Brāhmaṇa-kṣatriya-viśāṁ
śūdrāṇāṁ ca paraṁtapa /
karmāṇi pravibhaktāni
svabhāva-prabhavair guṇaih // 41

O great hero! The duties of Brāhmaṇas, Kṣatriyas, Vaiśyas and also of Śūdras have been divided according to the qualities born of their own nature.

Śamo damas tapaḥ śaucaṁ
kṣāntir ārjavam eva ca /

jñānaṁ vijñānam āstikyaṁ
brahma-karma svabhāva-jam // 42

Serenity, control of the senses, austerity, purity, straightforwardness, knowledge, insight, and faith in the Supreme Being — these are a Brāhmaṇa's duties born of his own nature.

Śauryaṁ tejo dhṛtir dākṣyaṁ
yuddhe c'āpy apalāyanam /
dānam īśvara-bhāvaś ca
kṣātraṁ karma svabhāva-jam // 43

Prowess, splendour of personality, unfailing courage, resourcefulness, dauntlessness in battle, generosity, leadership — these are a Kṣatriya's duties born of his own nature.

Kṛṣi-gaurakṣya-vāṇijyaṁ
vaiśya-karma svabhāva-jam /
paricary'ātmakaṁ karma
śūdrasy'āpi svabhāva-jam // 44

Agriculture, cattle-rearing and trade form the duty of the Vaiśya springing from his own nature, while the natural duty of a Śūdra consists in subordinate service under others.

Sve sve karmaṇy abhirataḥ
saṁsiddhiṁ labhate naraḥ /
sva-karma-nirataḥ siddhiṁ
yathā vindati tacchṛṇu // 45

By being devoted to one's own natural duty, man attains to spiritual competency. Now hear how devotion to one's own natural duty generates spiritual competency.

Yataḥ pravṛttir bhūtānāṁ
yena sarvaṁ idaṁ tatam /
sva-karmaṇā taṁ abhyarcya
siddhiṁ vindati mānavaḥ // 46

From whom all beings have emanated and by whom all this universe is pervaded — by worshipping Him through the dedicated performace of one's duty, man attains to spiritual competency (Siddhi).

Śreyān sva-dharmo viguṇaḥ
para-dharmāt svanuṣṭhitāt /
svabhāva-niyataṁ karma
kurvan n'āpnoti kilbiṣam // 47

One's own duty, even if without excellence (i.e. inferior) in the scale of worldly values, is more meritorious spiritually than the apparently well-performed duty of another. For, no sin is incurred by one doing works ordained according to one's nature (that is, in consonance with one's own natural evolution).

Sahajaṁ karma Kaunteya
sadoṣam api na tyajet /

sarv'ārambhā hi doṣeṇa
dhumen'āgnir iv'āvṛtāḥ // 48

O son of Kunti! Do not abandon the duty that is natural to you, even if some imperfections are incidental to it. For there is no undertaking without some imperfections, even as there is no fire without a covering of smoke.

Asakta-buddhiḥ sarvatra
jit'ātmā vigata-spṛhaḥ /
naiṣkarmya-siddhiṁ paramāṁ
saṁnyāsen'ādhigacchati // 49

Completely non-attached, self-subdued, and desireless, an aspirant attains the supreme perfection of transcendence of work through renunciation.

Siddhiṁ prāpto yathā Brahma
tath'āpnoti nibodha me /
samāsen'aiva Kaunteya
niṣṭhā jñānasya yā parā // 50

Now hear from Me in brief how one, who is established in the perfection of transcendence of work, attains to Brahman, the highest consummation of knowledge.

Buddhyā viśuddhayā yukto
dhṛtyā'tmānaṁ niyamya ca /
sabdādīn viṣayāṁs tyaktvā
rāga-dveṣau vyudasya ca //

Vivikta-sevī laghvāśī
yata-vāk-kāya-mānasaḥ /
dhyāna-yoga-paro nityaṁ
vairāgyaṁ samupāśritaḥ //

Ahaṁkāraṁ balaṁ darpaṁ
kāmaṁ krodhaṁ parigraham /
vimucya nirmamaḥ śānto
brahma-bhūyāya kalpate // 51-53

Endowed with a purifed intellect, established in self-control, abandoning the life of the senses as also attachments and antagonisms; frequenting solitary places, reducing food to the minimum; having speech, body and mind under control; ever meditative; endued with dispassion;

abandoning conceit, violence, lust, anger and possessiveness; selfless and tranquil, he becomes fit for beatification in Brahman - consciousness (Atman - consciousness).

Brahma-bhūtaḥ prasannātmā
na śocati na kāṅkṣati /
samaḥ sarveṣu bhūteṣu
mad-bhaktiṁ labhate parām // 54

Brahma-become (established in Ātman-Consciousness), tranquil in spirit, free from grief and passions, and regarding all beings alike, he gains supreme devotion to Me.

Bhaktyā mām abhijānānti
yāvān yaś-c'āsmi tattvataḥ /
tato māṁ tattvato jñātvā
viśate tad-anantaram // 55

By devotion does he come to know Me — both my extent and My essence. Knowing Me thus in truth and in reality, he enters into Me at once.

Sarva-karmāṇy api sadā
kurvāṇo mad-vyapāśrayaḥ /
mat-prasādād avāpnoti
śāśvataṁ padam avyayam // 56

Though performing every kind of work always, he who has taken refuge in Me shall, by My grace, attain to the eternal and indestructible state of Mokṣa (spiritual liberation).

Cetasā sarva-karmāṇi
mayi saṁnyasya mat-paraḥ /
buddhi-yogam upāśritya
mac-cittaḥ satataṁ bhava // 57

Mentally resigning all actions to Me (in respect of their fruits and agency), devoting yourself intensely to Me, and ever practising the communion of intellectual love, be you ever established in the thought of Me.

Mac-cittaḥ sarva-durgāṇi
mat-prasādāt tariṣyasi /
atha cet tvam ahaṁkārān
na śroṣyasi vinaṅkṣyasi // 58

If you are thus ever in communion with Me in mind, you will overcome every obstacle. But if, out of self-conceit, you do not listen to Me, destruction will be your fate.

Yad ahaṁkāram āśritya
na yotsya iti manyase /
mithy'aiṣa vyavasāyas te
prakṛtis tvāṁ niyokṣyati // 59

Vain is your resolve not to fight, born as it is of self-conceit. Nature will compel you.

Svabhāva-jena Kaunteya
nibaddhaḥ svena karmaṇā /
kartuṁ n'ecchasi yan mohāt
kariṣyasy avaśo'pi tat // 60

O son of Kunti! Duties which your natural tendencies have imposed upon you, but which out of delusion you refuse to do, even that you will have to perform by the compulsion of Nature.

Iśvaraḥ sarva-bhūtānāṁ
hṛd-deśe'rjuna tiṣṭhati /
bhrāmayan sarva-bhūtāni
yantr'ārūḍhāni māyayā // 61

O Arjuna! The Lord dwells in the heart of all beings revolving them all by His mysterious Power Māyā, as if they were objects mounted on a machine.

Tam eva śaraṇaṁ gaccha
sarva-bhāvena Bhārata /

tat-prasādāt parāṁ śāntiṁ
sthānaṁ prāpsyasi śāśvatam // 62

O scion of Bharata's clan! Seek refuge in Him, making a total surrender of your being — body, mind and soul. By His grace you shall attain to supreme peace and the everlasting abode.

Iti te jñānam ākhyātaṁ
guhyād guhyataraṁ mayā /
vimṛśy'aitad aśeṣeṇa
yath'ecchasi tathā kuru // 63

Thus have I imparted to you wisdom which is more secret (profound) than all that is secret (profound). Reflecting over this whole teaching, do as you think fit.

Sarva-guhyatamaṁ bhūyaḥ
śṛṇu me paramaṁ vacaḥ /
iṣṭo'si me dṛḍham iti
tato vakṣyāmi te hitam // 64

Listen again to My supreme word, the profoundest of all spiritual teachings. You are well beloved of Me; and so I shall tell you what is beneficial to you:

Man-manā bhava mad-bhakto
mad-yājī māṁ namas-kuru /
māṁ ev'aiṣyasi satyaṁ te
pratijāne priyo'si me // 65

Let your mind be engrossed in Me. Offer worship to Me. Be resigned to Me. Beloved as you are of me, I pledge in truth you shall come to Me alone.

Sarva-dharmān parityajya
māṁ ekaṁ śaraṇaṁ vraja /
ahaṁ tvā sarva-pāpebhyo
mokṣayiṣyāmi mā śucaḥ // 66

Abandoning (after sincere trial) dependence on all Dharmas (or human efforts at moral and spiritual upliftment), come to Me as the only Refuge. Grieve not; I will deliver you from all sins.

Idaṁ te n'ātapaskāya
n'ābhaktāya kadācana /

na c'āśuśrūṣave vācyaṁ
na ca māṁ yo'bhyasūyati // 67

This should on no account be imparted to those who do not practise austere living, who have no devotion to Me, who cavil at Me, and are devoid of the discipline of service.

Ya idam paramaṁ guhyaṁ
mad-bhakteṣv abhidhāsyati /
bhaktiṁ mayi parāṁ kṛtvā
mām ev'aiṣyaty asaṁśayaḥ // 68

He who teaches this supremely profound doctrine among men devoted to Me, having thereby offered to Me the highest form of loving service, shall undoubtedly come to Me alone.

Na ca tasmān manuṣyeṣu
kaścin me priya-kṛttamaḥ /
bhavitā na ca me tasmād
anyaḥ priyataro bhuvi // 69

No man can do anything more pleasing to Me than he, and nor shall any one on earth be dearer to Me than he.

Adhyeṣyate ca ya imaṁ
dharmyaṁ saṁvādam āvayoḥ /
jñāna-yajñena ten'āham
iṣṭaḥ syām iti me matiḥ // 70

It is My view that he who studies this conversation between us should be regarded as adoring Me with a sacrifice of knowledge.

Śraddhāvān anasūyaś ca
sṛṇuyād api yo naraḥ /
so'pi muktaḥ śubhān lokan
prāpnuyāt puṇya-karmaṇām // 71

Even a man who listens to this holy conversation between us with deep faith and receptivity shall attain to liberation and the happy regions open to righteous men.

Kaccid etac churtaṁ Pārtha
tvay'aik'āgreṇa cetasā /
kaccid ajñāna-sammohaḥ
praṇaṣtas te Dhanaṁjaya //72

Has this teaching been heard by you, O Arjuna, with a concentrated mind? Has all delusion born of ignorance been dispelled from you, O Dhananjaya?

Arjuna uvāca:

Naṣṭo mohaḥ smṛtir labdhā
tvat-prasādān mayā'cyuta /
sthito'smi gata-sandehaḥ
kariṣye vacanaṁ tava // 73

Arjuna said:

My delusion has been dispelled and my memory restored by Thy grace, O Undecaying Lord! I now stand firm, with all my doubts cleared, ready to execute Thy command.

Sañjaya uvāca:

Ity ahaṁ Vāsudevasya
Pārthasya ca mahātmanaḥ /
saṁvādam imam aśrauṣam
adbhutaṁ roma-harṣaṇam // 74

Sañjaya said:

Thus have I heard, with my hair standing on end, this wonderful conversation between Kṛṣṇa and the high-souled son of Pṛthā.

Vyāsa-prasādāc chrutavān
etad guhyam ahaṁ param /

yogaṁ yog'eśvārat kṛṣṇāt
sākṣāt kathayataḥ svayam // 75

Thus did I, by Vyāsa's grace, directly hear Kṛṣṇa, the Lord of Yoga, Himself teaching this Yoga, profound and supreme.

Rājan saṁsmṛtya-saṁsmṛtya
saṁvādam imam adbhutam /
Keśav'ārjunayoḥ puṇyaṁ
hṛṣyāmi ca muhur-muhuḥ // 76

Again and again, O king, does the memory of that sacred and astounding dialogue between Keśava and Arjuna come to my mind, causing no end of joy.

Tac ca saṁsmṛtya-saṁsmṛtya
rūpam atyadbhutaṁ Hareḥ /
vismayo me mahān rājan
hṛṣyāmi ca punaḥ-punaḥ // 77

Again and again does that most wondrous form of Hari arise in my mind, generating great astonishment and endless thrills of joy.

Yatra yog'eśvaraḥ Kṛṣṇo
yatra Pārtho dhanur-dharaḥ /
tatra śrīr vijayo bhūtir
dhrūvā nītir matir mama // 78

Wherever there is Kṛṣṇa, the Lord of Yoga, accompanied by Arjuna wielding the bow — there reign good fortune, victory, prosperity and sound policy. Such is my conviction.

Sri Kṛṣṇārpaṇam astu